PARODY

Parody is everywhere in contemporary modern culture. It runs through literature, theatre and television, architecture, film and even everyday speech. It is also at the heart of contemporary literary and cultural theory.

Drawing on examples from Aristophanes to *The Simpsons*, Simon Dentith explores the place of parody in the history of literature and introduces key controversies surrounding this mode of writing. He explores the subversive or conservative nature of parody and its pivotal role in recent postmodernist debate and, crucially, situates the form in the to-and-fro of linguistic and cultural exchange, from ancient times to the present.

Parody is a lively and engaging introduction to a crucial concept in contemporary literary and cultural studies, making even the most complex debates accessible to readers of all levels.

Simon Dentith is Reader in English at Cheltenham and Gloucester College of Higher Education. His publications include *Bakhtinian Thought: An Introductory Reader* (Routledge, 1995).

THE NEW CRITICAL IDIOM

SERIES EDITOR: JOHN DRAKAKIS, UNIVERSITY OF STIRLING

The New Critical Idiom is an invaluable series of introductory guides to today's critical terminology. Each book:

- provides a handy, explanatory guide to the use (and abuse) of the term
- offers an original and distinctive overview by a leading literary and cultural critic
- relates the term to the larger field of cultural representation

With a strong emphasis on clarity, lively debate and the widest possible breadth of examples, *The New Critical Idiom* is an indispensable approach to key topics in literary studies.

Also available in this series:

PARODY

Simon Dentith

LONDON AND NEW YORK

First published 2000
by Routledge
11 New Fetter Lane, London EC4P 4EE

Simultaneously published in the USA and Canada
by Routledge
29 West 35th Street, New York, NY 10001

Routledge is an imprint of the Taylor & Francis Group

© 2000 Simon Dentith

Typeset in Adobe Garamond and Scala Sans by
Taylor & Francis Books Ltd
Printed and bound in Great Britain by Clays Ltd, St Ives PLC

British Library Cataloguing in Publication Data
A catalogue record for this book is available from the British Library

Library of Congress Cataloging in Publication Data
Dentith, Simon.
Parody / Simon Dentith.
Includes bibliographical references.
1. Parody. I. Title.
PN6149.P3 D43 2000
809.7–dc21   99-088778

ISBN 0–415–18220–4 (hbk)
ISBN 0–415–18221–2 (pbk)

In memory of Jo Dentith (1917–1998),
who I hope would have enjoyed this book.

Contents

SERIES EDITOR'S PREFACE

The New Critical Idiom is a series of introductory books which seeks to extend the lexicon of literary terms, in order to address the radical changes which have taken place in the study of literature during the last decades of the twentieth century. The aim is to provide clear, well-illustrated accounts of the full range of terminology currently in use, and to evolve histories of its changing usage.

The current state of the discipline of literary studies is one where there is considerable debate concerning basic questions of terminology. This involves, among other things, the boundaries which distinguish the literary from the non-literary; the position of literature within the larger sphere of culture; the relationship between literatures of different cultures; and questions concerning the relation of literary to other cultural forms within the context of interdisciplinary studies.

It is clear that the field of literary criticism and theory is a dynamic and heterogeneous one. The present need is for individual volumes on terms which combine clarity of exposition with an adventurousness of perspective and a breadth of application. Each volume will contain as part of its apparatus some indication of the direction in which the definition of particular terms is likely to move, as well as expanding the disciplinary boundaries within which some of these terms have been traditionally contained. This will involve some re-situation of terms within the larger field of cultural representation, and will introduce examples from the area of film and the modern media in addition to examples from a variety of literary texts.

PREFACE

Thirty years ago, when John Jump wrote the volume *Burlesque* (1972) in the old 'Critical Idiom' series, discussion of parody played a minor, not to say disreputable, part in critical discourse. Jump, indeed, subsumed it under 'burlesque', which he took to be the generic word for the parodic forms. A long tradition of literary parody, especially prominent in the nineteenth century but persisting into the twentieth century also, had apparently marked the mode as irredeemably lightweight and second-order: in a more hostile vocabulary, as trivial and parasitic.

Two subsequent critical and cultural developments have given the study of parody a prominence it would have been hard for Jump and his contemporaries to imagine. First, the massive interest in the work of Mikhail Bakhtin (1895–1975) has placed parody, and the parodying forms more generally, at the heart of discussions about the history of writing, in the theatre and poetry as much as in the novel. Several strands of Bakhtin's various arguments are discussed in this book, while the closely related work in linguistics of his friend V.N. Vološinov provides one of its principal theoretical inspirations. However, although Bakhtin's rich legacy is one of my starting-points, I am by no means uncritical of some of the more one-sided accounts of parody that can be drawn from it; this book will attempt to demonstrate the profound ambivalence which has always characterised the mode.

Second, much of the controversy about the nature of postmodernism has turned on the place of parody in it, in architecture and literary writing, and in popular culture as well. These are highly contentious matters, and discussion of them leads into areas which are well beyond the scope of this book, concerning the nature of the global economy and indeed of contemporary civilisation. In an effort to keep the topic under control, I concentrate closely on the diverse cultural work performed by parody and the parodic forms, especially in contemporary literary culture; this leads me to a position which recognises the unusual prominence of such forms in the contemporary world, but which is also sceptical of claims that place parody, or the related form pastiche, at the heart of any new cultural dominant.

The pattern of the book broadly reflects these two critical developments. An introductory chapter places parody in the to-and-fro of linguistic interaction; while there is some discussion of definitions, the principal conclusion is that parody is but one name for a related group of forms that all intervene in different ways in the dialogues, conversations and dissensions that make up human discourse. A chapter devoted to the place of parody in ancient and medieval European culture is followed by three chapters which survey the part played by the parodic forms in the history of the novel, poetry and the drama. In all instances the emphasis is placed upon the substantive cultural work performed by parody, as it both inhibits and moves forward literary and cultural innovation. The final chapter takes on questions of parody and postmodernism, now visible in the context of a literary history which throws into relief the claims for novelty advanced on behalf of contemporary parodic forms.

ACKNOWLEDGEMENTS

It is a pleasure to acknowledge the help and encouragement of Peter Widdowson and Brean Hammond, who both found time from busy schedules to read substantial sections of this book. I am very grateful to them both. The general editor of the series, John Drakakis, has been supportive and encouraging throughout the book's composition; his editorial eye has also helped to shape the finished volume. I also wish to thank my family, who generally managed to refrain from parodying me as I began to find parody everywhere I looked. Finally, the book's dedication records my father, whose accents, now silent, were parodic and generous in equal measure.

I gratefully acknowledge permission for reprinting to the following:act from *The Waste Land*, from *Collected Poems, 1909–62*, by T.S. Eliot, London, Faber and Faber, 1963, reprinted by permission of the publisher.'The Lake Isle of Innisfree', from *Collected Poems*, by W.B. Yeats, London, Macmillan, 1950, reprinted by permission of A.P. Watt Ltd, and with the permission of Scribner, a Division of Simon & Schuster, from *The Collected Poems of W.B. Yeats*, Revised Second Edition by J. Finneran, copyright 1983, 1989 by Anne Yeats. 'Lake Isle', by Ezra Pound, from *Personae*, copyright 1926 by Ezra Pound, reprinted by permission of New Directions Publishing Corp., and Faber and Faber. 'A Nursery Rhyme, as it might have been written by T.S. Eliot', from *Making Cocoa for Kingsley Amis*, by Wendy Cope, London, Faber and Faber, 1986, reprinted by permission of the publisher. Extract from 'Chard Whitlow', from *Collected Poems* by Henry Reed, edited by Jon Stallworthy, Oxford, Oxford University Press, 1991, reprinted by permission of Oxford University Press. 'From *The Waste Land*', from *Poems Not on the Underground*, by Roger Tagholm, published by the Windrush Press Ltd, 1996, reprinted by permission of the publisher. Extract from 'Learnt Torsions', from *The Literary Labyrinth*, by Bernard Sharratt, Brighton, The Harvester Press, 1984, reprinted by permission of the author. Extracts from *Possession*, by A.S. Byatt, London, Chatto & Windus, 1990, reprinted by permission of the publisher.

many discursive interactions are characterised by the imitation and repetition, derisive or otherwise, of another's words. Imitation is the way in which we learn to speak, taking in, as we do so, not merely a grammar and a vocabulary, but a whole repertoire of manners, attitudes, and ways of speaking. Parodic imitation of another's words is merely one possibility among the whole range of rejoinders that make up human discourse, and parodic imitation can itself take many forms. Listening to the language of children and adolescents (and not only them), you will hear a multitude of parodies, as accents are mocked, oral styles from the television are attempted, fashionable phrases are tried on or discarded, so that each of a whole panoply of verbal and cultural styles is in turn derided or assumed. The slang of one generation becomes the target of parody in the next: 'hip' and 'ace' are long since as comic as 'ripping' and 'jolly good', and to use them would be to make yourself subject to mocking laughter.

It is in discourse, understood in this way as a never-ending to-and-fro of rejoinders, that our understanding of the practice of parody should initially be situated. In this context, parody is but one of the ways in which the normal processes of linguistic interaction proceed. For to speak a language is much more than merely to have a command of its grammar and vocabulary. It entails using these resources to adopt an evaluative attitude – both to the person to whom one speaks, and to the topic of discussion. Thus in addressing those to whom we speak, we take up, willy-nilly, attitudes which, in many different ways, reinforce or contradict our addressees. Equally, we indicate in a thousand verbal ways a particular stance to whatever it is that we are talking about. These attitudes are carried in part by *intonation*, an aspect of language unique to each individual utterance and its occasion. So as we speak we necessarily indicate our attitude to that about which we speak, and towards those to whom we speak: by tone of voice, by the adoption or otherwise of the appropriate politeness conventions, by register and diction, by fitting or unfitting adaptation of speech to occasion. These means permit a remarkable array of attitudes to become apparent in our speech – of complaint or reluctant consent, of eager or truculent agreement, of celebration, of irony, of private reservation, or indeed of any of a hundred such attitudes. Parody, be it of the interlocutor's speech, or of the speech of some third party, or even of oneself, is one of the ways in which these inevitable evaluations occur. Its simplest form is perhaps the scoffing repetition illustrated in *Middlemarch*, also a familiar feature of childish argument, by which even the most innocent phrase can be mocked and made to sound ridiculous:

SPEAKER 1:   'I don't like this cold weather.'
SPEAKER 2:   (*in exaggeratedly feeble and whining tones*) *'I don't like this cold weather.'*

In many more sophisticated ways, and in some less conscious ways also, we respond evaluatively to what is said to us; parody is but one possibility among many.

There is a further, and fundamental, way in which the apparently specialised use of language that we call parody can be related to more general characteristics of language. At some level – later this will be specified more exactly – parody involves the imitation and transformation of another's words. That might also pass as an account of language use more generally, for language is not one's own, but always comes to each speaker from another, to be imitated and transformed as that speaker in turn sends it onwards. All utterances are part of a chain, and as they pass through that chain they acquire particular valuations and intonations on each occasion of their use. In this most general sense, we are all condemned to parody, for we can do no more than parrot another's word as it comes to be our turn to speak it.

Yet this is not a conclusion in which I wish to rest, albeit that it usefully indicates the potential scope of a comprehensive account of the topic of parody. We can certainly do more than speak parrot-fashion; and the example of Mr Brooke's parodist suggests that when we do, it has a very disturbing effect on the utterance that we repeat. Rather, as we use language – necessarily not our own – to a greater or lesser degree we *make* it our own. So while all language use certainly involves imitation, the particular inflection that we give to that imitation (and parody is one possible inflection) indicates the extent to which we have adapted language to occasion, transformed the value given to the utterance, and thus redirected the evaluative direction in that chain of utterances. Parody is one of the means available to us to achieve all these ends.

The general account of language in which I have just situated the practice of parody is based upon that of the Russian linguistician V.N. Vološinov, whose account of language is closely related to that of his fellow-Russian, Mikhail Bakhtin. One of the distinctive features of Vološinov's theory of language is that it stresses the priority of *speech*; certainly for both him and Bakhtin (whose theories of parody will play an important part in this book) the speech situation and a theory of the *utterance* form the essential basis for their understanding of all language uses, including written ones. I will follow their lead in seeking to understand the particularities of *writing* by drawing on an understanding of language derived from the spoken interchanges that constitute it. There are many difficulties in such an attitude, principally to do with the ephemeral nature of speech compared with the permanent nature of writing; and since the parodies that I will be discussing in this book are mostly written ones, I do not wish to underestimate these difficulties. Nevertheless, I propose to leave them to one side for the moment in order to suggest how we might understand written parodies in terms of the chain of utterances and the evaluative attitude necessarily adopted by every interlocutor in that chain.

One designation, for written discourse, of what Vološinov

describes for speech as 'the chain of utterances', is *intertextuality*. This can be characterised initially as the interrelatedness of writing, the fact that all written utterances – texts – situate themselves in relation to texts that precede them, and are in turn alluded to or repudiated by texts that follow. Indeed, there is a tradition of specific 'rejoinder poems', closely related to more formal parodies, in which 'answering back' is especially visible – Sir Walter Raleigh's 'The Nymph's Reply to the Shepherd' (1600), which is a response to Christopher Marlowe's 'The Passionate Shepherd to His Love' (*ca.* 1590), is a famous example of such poems. But there is also a less specific form of answering back, as when the seventeenth-century libertine poet Rochester begins one of his lyrics 'Tell me no more of constancy ...'; in this instance he is making an intertextual allusion to a presumed discourse in praise of constancy which precedes the poem and which he is repudiating. Intertextuality includes more profound aspects of writing than this, however. At the most obvious level it denotes the myriad *conscious* ways in which texts are alluded to or cited in other texts: the dense network of quotation, glancing reference, imitation, polemical refutation and so on in which all texts have their being. At a still more profound level, intertextuality refers to the dense web of allusion out of which individual texts are constituted – their constant and inevitable use of ready-made formulations, catch phrases, slang, jargon, cliché, commonplaces, unconscious echoes, and formulaic phrases. All these linguistic echoes and repetitions are accented in variously evaluative ways, as they are subjected – or not – to overt ridicule, or mild irony, or in the expectation that the repetition of the bureaucratic phrase of the month will gain the writer credit, and so forth. This aspect of intertextuality is more visible in some kinds of writing than in others. Tabloid journalese, for example, or the diction of neoclassical poetry, are both noticeably formulaic, though of course different writers of these genres can put their formulae to very diverse uses. My contention is simply this:

that parody is one of the many forms of intertextual allusion out of which texts are produced.

In this sense, parody forms part of a range of cultural practices, which allude, with deliberate evaluative intonation, to precursor texts. Just as we cannot speak without adopting an attitude towards those to whom we speak, and towards that about which we speak, so also we must situate ourselves evaluatively towards the language that we use. The relevant range of cultural practices could conveniently be arranged as a spectrum, according to the evaluations that differing forms make of the texts that they cite, with reverential citation at one end of the scale ('My text today is taken from ...'), to hostile parody at the other end, and passing through a multitude of cultural forms on the way. Thus the spectrum would include imitation, pastiche, mock-heroic, burlesque, travesty, spoof, and parody itself. I hesitate to set out this scale in too formal a way, however, for a number of reasons. In the first place, all such classifications of cultural forms tend to invite analyses of texts of a reductively pigeon-holing kind. Second, the discussion of parody is bedevilled by disputes over definition, a fruitless form of argument unless there are matters of substance at stake – of genuine differences of cultural politics, for example. Finally, because of the antiquity of the word parody (it is one of the small but important group of literary-critical terms to have descended from the ancient Greeks), because of the range of different practices to which it alludes, and because of differing national usages, no classification can ever hope to be securely held in place. So for the time being I will affirm that parody in writing, like parody in speech, is part of the everyday processes by which one utterance alludes to or takes its distance from another; and that there are a number of adjacent forms which do the same, while there are equally many other forms which make allusions for quite opposite evaluative purposes. All this is part of the intertextual constitution and competition of writing.

We can use the notion of intertextuality to help us still further in situating and characterising parody. Developing that distinction between different kinds of intertextuality – between the deliberate and explicit allusion to a precursor text or texts, on the one hand, and a more generalised allusion to the constitutive codes of daily language, on the other – allows us to distinguish between different kinds of parody. One distinction often made is between 'specific' and 'general' parody, the former aimed at a specific precursor text, the latter at a whole body of texts or kind of discourse. Thus Lewis Carroll's poem 'How Doth the Little Crocodile' ('How doth the little crocodile/Improve his shining tail ...') is a *specific* parody of Isaac Watts's poem 'Against Idleness and Mischief' ('How does the little busy bee/Improve each shining hour ...'). By contrast, Cervantes' novel *Don Quixote* is a *general* parody of the chivalric romance as a genre. This distinction neatly correlates with that which I have drawn between intertextual modes. However, we can use the distinction in modes to capture another aspect of parody, between the fully developed formal parody which constitutes the complete text – whose whole *raison d'être* is its relation to its precursor text or parodied mode – and those glancing parodic allusions which are to be found very widely in writing, often aimed at no more than a phrase or fragment of current jargon and sometimes indicated by little more than 'scare quotes' (the written equivalent of a hostile intonation).

Thus in the following paragraph from *Bleak House*, Dickens makes a whole series of parodic allusions, without having any specific precursor text in mind. The death of one of the characters in the novel has caused a stir of activity:

> Next day the court is all alive – is like a fair, as Mrs. Perkins, more than reconciled to Mrs. Piper, says, in amiable conversation with that excellent woman. The Coroner is to sit in the first-floor room at the Sol's Arms, where the Harmonic Meetings take place twice a week, and where the chair is filled by a gentleman of professional celebrity,

faced by Little Swills, the comic vocalist, who hopes (according to the bill in the window) that his friends will rally round him, and support first-rate talent. The Sol's Arms does a brisk stroke of business all the morning. Even children so require sustaining, under the general excitement, that a pieman, who has established himself for the occasion at the corner of the court, says his brandy-balls go off like smoke. What time the beadle, hovering between the door of Mr. Krook's establishment and the door of the Sol's Arms, shows the curiosity in his keeping to a few discreet spirits, and accepts the compliment of a glass of ale or so in return.

(Dickens, 1971–3: Chapter 11)

Dickens's parodic references here, marked with varying evaluative charges, are all allusions, not to any specific precursor text, but more to particular phraseologies, even to what can only be described as a tone of voice. The various languages that circulate around the court (that is, some of the dialects of working-class London), reappear here in mildly parodied form. Much of the paragraph is in 'double-voiced discourse', so that we can hear in the writing simultaneous traces both of the characters' speech and the author's attitude towards it. Thus we can hear in the extract the accents of Mrs. Perkins and Mrs. Piper ('that excellent woman'), the jargon of semi-professional entertainment, the slang of the pieman, and the pomposity of the beadle ('accepts the compliment of a glass of ale'). It is helpful to see, in the pervasiveness of parody in a characteristically Dickensian paragraph such as this, an indication of the author's multitudinous recycling of the diverse languages of mid-nineteenth-century English. Writing of this kind marks one limit of what might count as parody, making scarcely hostile allusions to what are little more than the slightly inflected phrases of contemporary speech. The passage nevertheless indicates the potential scope of parody, if it is understood as one form of the more general intertextual constitution of all writing.

I am therefore moving towards a wide and inclusive account of parody, rather than a narrowly formal one. The definition of parody that I am about to offer is based, not on any specific formal or linguistic features, but on the intertextual stance that writing adopts. Accordingly, I conclude this section with this preliminary definition of parody: 'Parody includes any cultural practice which provides a relatively polemical allusive imitation of another cultural production or practice'.

In order to capture the evaluative aspect of parody, I include the word 'polemical' in the definition; this word is used to allude to the contentious or 'attacking' mode in which parody can be written, though it is 'relatively' polemical because the ferocity of the attack can vary widely between different forms of parody. And finally, in a distinction whose importance is about to become clearer, the direction of the attack can vary. So far I have been stressing the importance of parody as *rejoinder*, or mocking response to the word of another. But many parodies draw on the authority of precursor texts to attack, satirise, or just playfully to refer to elements of the contemporary world. These parodies also need to be reckoned in to any definition, so the polemical direction of parody can draw on the allusive imitation to attack, not the precursor text, but some new situation to which it can be made to allude. Such parodies, indeed, are the stock in trade of innumerable compilations of light and comic verse and of literary competitions, and their 'polemical' content is often very slight indeed.

DEFINITIONS

Given the often humorous and anti-academic nature of parody, it is ironic that discussions of the topic have been bedevilled by academic disputes about definition. What exactly did the ancient Greeks mean by 'parodia'? How can we distinguish, in a hard and fast way, between parody, travesty, and pastiche? Does parody necessarily have a polemical relationship to the parodied text? It

is partly because of these disputes that I have drawn my definition of parody in as wide-ranging a way as possible, and have
based it upon linguistic interaction, both verbal and written. On
this basis, some of the disputes about definition which we are
about to review briefly will seem less significant, though they
will point eventually to a large question about the cultural politics of parody, namely whether it is to be thought of as an essentially conservative or essentially subversive mode − indeed, we
shall have to ask whether it is possible to talk of parody as 'essentially' anything at all.

Aristotle's *Poetics* provides the earliest use of the word *parodia*
(παρῳδία), where he uses it to refer to the earlier writer Hegemon.
A *parodia* is a narrative poem, of moderate length, in the metre
and vocabulary of epic poems, but treating a light, satirical, or
mock-heroic subject (the epic poems familiar to the Greeks were
those of Homer, the *Iliad* and the *Odyssey*; mock-heroic, a form
related to parody, applies the idiom of epic poetry to everyday or
'low' subjects, to comic effect). A *parodia* is a specific literary
form for which prizes were awarded at poetic contests; only one of
these poems, the *Batrachomyomachia*, or *Battle of the Frogs and
Mice*, has survived. However, this is not the only meaning of the
word in Greek and subsequent Roman writers, who also use the
term and its grammatical cognates to refer to a more widespread
practice of quotation, not necessarily humorous, in which both
writers and speakers introduce allusions to previous texts. Indeed,
this is a more frequent use of the term (Householder, 1944: 1–9).
Aristophanes's allusions, in his comedies, to the tragedies of
Euripides are a special case of such parodic quotations. However,
the case of Aristophanes points to one of the difficulties surrounding the definition of *parodia*, namely whether the term had
any polemical edge to it in classical Greece, since there is controversy over whether the comic playwright was or was not attacking his tragic contemporary. Certainly, we must recognise that
the Greek uses of the term do not simply correspond with mod-

ern English usage, where some sense of parody mocking the parodied text is at least usual. Thus there is apparently no evidence
that the *parodia*, meaning the mock-heroic poem, ever mocked
Homer rather than imitated him for comic effect. For such mocking or carnivalesque forms, we should turn instead to the satyr
plays which accompanied performances of Greek tragic drama.
However, we can recognise that Greek usage, in its extension to a
more widespread practice of quotation or allusion, does license
my more inclusive definition, since the word in its related forms
includes not only the specific *parodia* to which Aristotle refers,
but also a wider practice of allusion and quotation.

The term 'parodia' has subsequently had a long and complicated
history, acquiring differing connotations as the artistic practices
to which it has been made to refer have themselves altered. These
different meanings in part spring, also, from varying national traditions. I shall discuss here four recent accounts of parody which
all offer competing definitions. The point is not to adjudicate
between them, but to see whether it is possible to assimilate
these definitions to the account of parody, based upon linguistic
and written interaction, that I have offered.

I start with what is surely the most comprehensive survey of
the different modes of intertextuality, namely *Palimpsestes* (1982)
by the French literary theorist Gerard Genette, a book which can
represent all attempts to offer hard and fast distinctions between
the various kinds of parody – travesty, burlesque, and so on. The
most striking feature of Genette's account is that it seeks to produce a classification of these cultural forms based on the differing
formal relations between texts. The result is to produce a very
tight definition of parody, distinguishing it carefully from the
related forms of travesty, transposition, pastiche, skit and forgery.
Thus parody is to be distinguished from travesty because the textual transformation which it performs is done in a playful rather
than a satirical manner. Pastiche, on the other hand, is similarly
playful, but works by imitation rather than direct transformation.

Skits (French: *charges*) are doubly unlike parodies in that they work both by imitation and in a satirical regime.

What are the consequences of these careful formal distinctions? Using English examples rather than the French ones used by Genette, we can consider the following cases. Lewis Carroll's 'You are old, Father William' remains a parody, because it is a transformation of Southey's poem performed in a playful way. Here is Southey's poem, 'The old man's comforts':

> You are old, Father William, the young man cried,
> The few locks which are left you are grey;
> You are hale, Father William, a hearty old man,
> Now tell me the reason, I pray.
>
> In the days of my youth, Father William replied,
> I remember'd that youth would fly fast,
> And abused not my health and my vigour at first,
> That I never might need them at last.
>
> (Southey, 1909: 385–6)

And now here is Lewis Carroll's parody:

> 'You are old, Father William,' the young man said,
> 'And your hair it is growing quite white;
> And yet you persistently stand on your head –
> Do you think, at your age, it is right?'
>
> 'In my youth,' Father William replied to his son,
> 'I feared it might injure the brain;
> But now that I'm perfectly sure I have none,
> Why, I do it again and again.'
>
> (Jerrold and Leonard, 1913: 309)

In Genette's terms, this is exactly a parody, since the 'hypertext' (Carroll's poem) directly transforms the 'hypotext' (Southey's poem) in a playful way – though we should perhaps note that there is a mild polemical intention in Carroll's parody, towards the smug didacticism of the parodied text. In passing, we can note the usefulness of these terms 'hypotext' and 'hypertext', the former denoting the preceding or original text upon which the latter, the hypertext, performs its parodic transformation.

Henry Fielding's *Shamela* (1741), on the other hand, is not to be described as a parody according to Genette, because though it directly transforms its hypotext, Richardson's *Pamela* (1740), it does so in a satirical rather than a playful regime. It is therefore, in this classification, a travesty. Certainly Fielding's satirical purpose is evident enough in *Shamela*, since his aim is to debunk what he takes to be the hypocrisy and prurience of Richardson's text. As an example of pastiche, we can mention Pope's mock-heroic poem *The Rape of the Lock* (1714), which imitates epic verse without direct transformation of it, in a generally playful way. And finally, as a skit or *charge*, we can bring forward those innumerable literary games in which players are asked to produce a piece of writing 'in the manner of' a particular writer, where there is no direct transformation of the writer's work, but a general imitation in a satirical regime. Here is an example; players in a *New Statesman* competition were asked to rewrite an incident from the Bible in the manner of a writer of their choice, so this is the story of the loaves and fishes in the manner of Irvine Welsh, author of *Trainspotting* (1993):

> -The crowd wants nosh, man. And so do I. Philip patted his belly.
> Jesus snorted.-You don't look like you needed any.
> -They can fuck off and buy their own, I said.
> -There's no shops here, said Andrew.-Soon they'll faint.
> -Bugger that said Jesus.-Let's see what we've got.
> Andrew went round with a basket.
> -That's pathetic, I said.-Two fishes and five loaves? That's IT?
> -SEVEN loaves, DICKHEAD!
> -You an IDIOT, or what? You've got five there!

-Shut the FUCK UP, said Jesus. He waved his hand over the basket
-Hocus ... Pocus ...

(Keizer, 1998: 53)

The humour of this derives from the extreme distance between sacred topic and the violent urban slang, 'in the manner of' Irvine Welsh, in which the story is conducted (though it might be thought to be pretty tame Welsh, with a very low obscenity count per sentence). There is no direct transformation of Welsh's prose, but a satirical imitation of it, justifying its inclusion under the heading of skit rather than parody.

The value of this kind of distinction, however, is ultimately limited. It certainly has the merit of focusing attention on the specific formal operations that the hypertexts perform, and provides some useful vocabulary for describing them. But it suffers from the difficulty of attempting to reform or reconstitute a whole vocabulary by an act of scholarly *force majeure*, as though habitual usage could be single-handedly transformed in the name of greater precision. More seriously, the chief merit of Genette's work – the construction of a classification based on formally distinguished textual operations – is also its principal disadvantage. In the context of a more general account of parody as a possible mode of linguistic or textual interaction, Genette's account is helpful in focusing on the diverse textual operations that can characterise that interaction, but loses sight of the social and historical ground in which that interaction occurs, and the evaluative and ideological work performed by parody.

A very different account of parody is offered by Margaret Rose in *Parody/Metafiction: An Analysis of Parody as a Critical Mirror to the Writing and Reception of Fiction* (1979) and *Parody: Ancient, Modern and Post-modern* (1993). In the former book especially, Rose argues that certain kinds of parodic fiction act as metafictions – i.e., that in parodying one text (or kind of text), the parody text holds up a mirror to its own fictional practices, so that it is at once a fiction and a fiction *about* fictions. Furthermore, Rose addresses the paradox that, while apparently being destructive, parody texts actually create new fictions out of their own parodic procedures. This is an argument that works especially well for the great classic novels which are in part built out of parody – *Don Quixote*, *Tristram Shandy* and *Ulysses* – for in all these instances the presence of parody draws attention to the conventions that constitute narrative and novel-writing. Thus Rose's analysis of parody is especially strong in drawing attention to the negotiations that are involved in *reading* a parody text, as the reader's expectations are disrupted and adjustments are required.

This account of parody can thus be compared with that offered by Robert Phiddian, in *Swift's Parody* (1995). The metafictional consequence of parody, detected by Rose, takes on here a more properly deconstructive colouring; in other words, Phiddian extends the argument from one in which the parodic text is a fiction *about* other fictions to an argument which suggests that parody throws some of the very fundamentals of writing into doubt. Following the French theorist Roland Barthes' notion of the 'death of the author', parody emerges as a formal practice in which the densely allusive intertextual nature of all writing is made especially transparent, so that its 'authorship' becomes problematic. At least, that is how Phiddian characterises some aspects of Swift's *A Tale of a Tub* (1704). He can then move on from Barthes to the philosopher Jacques Derrida; Phiddian seeks to use his notion of 'writing under erasure' (by which is suggested the impossibility of doing without the very words one recognises as inadequate) as a metaphor for the activity of parody:

> The application of this metaphor to the perception of parody is obvious enough: all parody refunctions pre-existing text(s) and/or discourses, so it can be said that these verbal structures are called to the readers' minds and then placed under erasure. A necessary modification of the original idea is that we must allow the act of erasure to

operate critically rather than as merely neutral cancellation of its object. Parodic erasure disfigures its pre-texts in various ways that seek to guide our re-evaluation or refiguration of them. It is dialogical and suggestive as well as negatively deconstructive, for it (at least potentially) can achieve controlled and meta-fictional commentary as well as purely arbitrary problematisation.

(Phiddian, 1995: 13–14)

This is suggestive, and need not be applied rigorously; Phiddian wishes to use the metaphorical implications of the notion of 'writing under erasure' to suggest the multiple ways in which parody can invite the reader to examine, evaluate and re-situate the hypotextual material.

Both these accounts, that of Rose as much as Phiddian's, seem to me persuasive within their own terms; that is, they are persuasive accounts of the texts with which they deal, and draw eloquent attention to some of the perceptual consequences of the parodic acts that those texts perform. However, it is important not to take them as general accounts of parody; not *all* parodies act in metafictional or deconstructive ways, but *some* do. They deal with one moment of the parodic act – the perceptual consequences to the reader – and leave implicit the location of that parodic act within the wider rhetorical situation. But they also point to one important function of parody, which is the act of implicit criticism that it performs. I shall return to this critical function later.

Finally, I turn to Linda Hutcheon's account of parody in *A Theory of Parody: The Teachings of Twentieth-Century Art Forms* (1985). Hutcheon is averse to offering any trans-historical definition of parody, concentrating instead on the ways that certain twentieth-century art forms offer parodic allusions to the art of the past. Working from this material, she concludes that it is wrong to define parody by its polemical relation to the parodied text (the hypotext, in Genette's terms), since many of the contemporary art works that she discusses simply do not have that polemical edge to them. Indeed, the neoclassical practice of 'imitation' would be an illuminating parallel for the kind of parody she analyses, since this form characteristically seeks to rewrite an admired classical original in contemporary terms in order to draw upon its authority and to gain purchase upon the modern world. Here, then, is an account of parody which appears to challenge the definition that I have given of the mode, in which the polemical nature of the parodic allusion is central.

However, I believe that Hutcheon's account, strongly based, as it is, on a particular artistic practice, can be assimilated to my preliminary definition because the polemic can work both ways: towards the imitated text or towards the 'world'. Thus it is certainly true, even taking familiar literary examples, that parody does not have to have a polemical relation to the texts that are 'quoted'. For example, in section III of *The Waste Land*, Eliot makes a parodic allusion to Spenser's 'Prothalamion':

> The river's tent is broken; the last fingers of leaf
> Clutch and sink into the wet bank. The wind
> Crosses the brown land, unheard. The nymphs are departed.
> Sweet Thames, run softly till I end my song.
> The river bears no empty bottles, sandwich papers,
> Silk handkerchiefs, cardboard boxes, cigarette ends
> Or other testimony of summer nights. The nymphs are departed.
> And their friends, the loitering heirs of city directors;
> Departed, have left no addresses.
> By the waters of Leman I sat down and wept ...
> Sweet Thames, run softly till I end my song,
> Sweet Thames, run softly, for I speak not loud or long.
> But at my back in a cold blast I hear
> The rattle of the bones, and chuckle spread from ear to ear.
>
> (Eliot, 1963: 70)

Compare Spenser's poem, which gives a highly coloured account of the Thames and the nymphs who are gathering flowers on its banks, and whose stanzas all conclude:

> Against the Bridall day, which is not long:
> Sweet Thames, run softly till I end my song.

Eliot's parody of Spenser has as its polemical target not the 'Prothalamion', but the contemporary (1920s') state of the Thames, London, and indeed civilisation. Spenser's poem provides Eliot with a kind of standard by which to measure the ugliness of the modern world, and the benign bridal song of the hypotext measures the sordidness of 1920s' sexual relations, indicated by the detritus that flows down the river, including 'other testimony of summer nights', about which readers do not wish to enquire too closely. This is the predominant direction of the parody in the poem: using Spenser to belittle the contemporary world. It may be, however, that some of Eliot's sexual scepticism about 1920s' London seeps back to Spenser's poem, which does not remain uncontaminated by its association with *The Waste Land*. Despite this possibility, it is clear that, overwhelmingly, the parody is polemically directed towards the world, and it draws on the authority of the parodied text to establish its own evaluative stance.

The question is, therefore, whether we say that this text, and others like it, is best not thought of as a parody (which would be Genette's solution), or whether we stretch the definition of parody to include texts like *The Waste Land* and the artistic examples brought forward by Hutcheon. My inclusive definition certainly inclines me to the latter solution; that is, that the polemical allusive imitation of a preceding text that characterises parody can have its polemic directed to the world rather than the preceding text. However, in saying this we must also recognise that 'parody' now alludes to a spectrum of cultural practices and the specific ways in which individual parodies work will always require careful elucidation.

This sense of a 'spectrum' or continuum of cultural practices is perhaps the most important conclusion to be drawn from this brief survey of definitions. 'Parody' should be thought of, not as a single and tightly definable genre or practice, but as a range of cultural practices which are all more or less parodic. Thus in this book I will as often refer to 'parodic cultural forms' as to parody in the singular. The range of available parodic forms (and the names that they go under) varies dramatically from period to period, in a way that challenges any schema of definitions. However, it is possible to recognise a continuum of parodic cultural work or parodic cultural effects, within which different texts (or even different moments within the same text) can be situated. The spectrum of parodic forms, as Genette's book indicates, will include such varying matters as the extent and closeness of the imitation, the degree of hostility, and the play between 'high' and 'low' (of manner and matter) which the parody sets in motion. But these varying practices are used with differing prominence at different periods and go under different names when they are used.

Hutcheon's examples, and the account of parody that they lead to, point us eventually to some of the most contentious aspects of our topic. For they concern the respect or otherwise with which parodied texts are treated, and around this issue gathers the large question of the cultural politics of parody. If one includes under 'parody' texts that make respectful allusions to precursor texts in order to take a polemical attitude to the world, then one is unlikely to see the activity of parody as a predominantly subversive one. Conversely, if one restricts parody to those texts which take a negatively evaluative attitude to the parodied text, one is more likely to see parody in these terms, though there is also the possibility that parody can be used to attack, not the texts of authority, but whatever is new, unusual, or threatening to the status quo. Indeed, another of Hutcheon's books, *Irony's Edge* (1994), suggests an instructive parallel for these latter alternatives. In that book, Hutcheon documents two rival accounts of irony. In one tradition, irony is seen as essentially conservative, destroying the seriousness required to transform society, and reconciling its inhabitants to a world of second bests. 'Which of us is happy in this world? Which of us has his desires? or, having it, is satisfied?', asks Thackeray at the end of *Vanity Fair*, and his question could be taken as a type of the ironic attitude according to this tradition. By contrast, there is an alternative tradition in which irony is seen as essentially subversive, unsettling the certainties which sustain the social order, and placing all final truths under suspension. A comparable set of alternatives have characterised reflection on parody. On the one hand, it has been seen as conservative in the way that it is used to mock literary and social innovation, policing the boundaries of the sayable in the interests of those who wish to continue to say what has always been said. On the other hand, there is another tradition which celebrates the subversive possibilities of parody as its essential characteristic; parody in this view typically attacks the official word, mocks the pretensions of authoritative discourse, and undermines the seriousness with which subordinates should approach the justifications of their betters.

These matters of definition, then, take us into some broader questions. However, there is nothing in them which requires us to abandon our initial characterisation of parody as any cultural practice which makes a polemical allusive imitation of another cultural production or practice, though we have to recognise that this definition points to a range of specific forms which require more careful specification in practice. Since all four accounts start from different examples of parodies, drawn from diverse periods and cultures, it is not surprising that they point towards conflicting definitions of parody. Indeed, this diversity is partly explicable if these definitions are seen as alluding to differing phases or emphases within a related band of parodistic cultural interactions – that is, each definition tends to offer as the *essential* characteristic an aspect which is better thought of as a phase only of parody when it is understood in the fullness of its discursive situation. It is this emphasis on 'practice' with which I conclude this section, for it directs us towards some of those broader questions of cultural politics, and the historical specificity of parody, which form the topic of the following discussion.

A HISTORY OF PARODY?

One obvious difficulty about any account of parody which is based, like mine, upon a general account of language, is that it is difficult for it to cope with the historically specific forms of parody that have been produced over the ages. Can any such general description accommodate practices as diverse as the Greek Old Comedy of Aristophanes, the ancient literary form known as the menippea (a genre of self-parodying serio-comic writing), medieval *parodia sacra* or parody of sacred texts, the tradition within the modern novel from *Don Quixote* to *Vanity Fair* for which parody is an essential component, the genre of literary parody in the nineteenth century which culminates in Beerbohm's *A Christmas Garland* (1912), and so-called postmodernism in which parody plays a crucial role? This range of material certainly seems too wide to be accommodated in any single definition, and any attempt to do so would seem to strip all these various cultural practices of their specific purchase on the differing historical worlds that they emerge from and speak to.

There are in fact several different problems concealed within this general difficulty. The first concerns the very nature of the universalising description of language upon which my account of parody depends. Following Vološinov and Bakhtin, I make the presumption that language is a way both of realising and conducting social relations; since all human societies have been characterised by greater or lesser degrees of social conflict, I take it that the conditions for linguistic evaluations and revaluations have always existed. This is to say nothing about the particular ways in which parodic forms have operated in particular social situations. 'Parody', in this sense, is as much a universal as 'response' or 'intonation'.

Nevertheless, there is a problem with the historicity of parody. If it is a general feature of discursive situations, is it possible to describe it in ways that pay due attention to its historical conditions of possibility? In the chapters that follow, I argue that parody has flourished at particular historical moments, and I shall give more detailed accounts of some of them. It is worth asking whether any particular set of historical circumstances leads parody to flourish, and whether, conversely, in other situations it withers away. For example, given the efflorescence of parody in places like medieval monasteries and Universities, and in modern British public (i.e. private) schools, is parody more likely to be produced in closed social situations such as these? Alternatively, does the prevalence of parody in the relatively democratic social situation of ancient Athens, or the fluid and turbulent societies of Early Modern Europe, suggest that it flourishes better in 'open' social formations?

These questions are important, ultimately, because the answers to them bear upon the cultural politics of parody. We can give more substance to the alternatives sketched in above. The broadly 'subversive' account of parody is most fully expressed in the work of one of the most influential cultural theorists of the twentieth century, Mikhail Bakhtin, whom we have already encountered in relation to his theories of language. Actually, it is incorrect to attribute to him a specific theory of parody, since his account of parody emerges as part of a more general characterisation of 'carnival' and the 'carnivalesque', which he advanced especially in his book on the French sixteenth-century comic novelist, François Rabelais, *Rabelais and His World* (1984b). For Bakhtin, parody is just one of the cultural forms that draw upon the popular energies of the carnival. In late medieval and Early Modern Europe especially, he argues, the popular institution of the carnival, with its feasting, its celebratory enactments of the overthrowing of authority, and its militantly anti-authoritarian debunking of sacred and official rituals and languages, provides the social ground for the grotesque realism, mimicries, multiple registers, and parodies to be found in Rabelais and his near-contemporaries Cervantes and Shakespeare. Following Bakhtin, parody indeed emerges from a particular set of social and historical circumstances; it is mobilised to debunk official seriousness, and to testify to the relativity of all languages, be they the dialects of authority or the jargons of guilds, castes or priesthoods.

This is an inspiriting notion of parody, which has especial force for the Early Modern period, but has relevance also to other eras, where the actual institution of carnival is notably absent, such as ancient Greece or nineteenth-century England. For the notion of the 'carnivalesque' can be extended to include all those cultural situations where the authority of a single language of authority is called into question, notably by the simultaneous co-presence of other languages which can challenge it. One principal method by which such challenges are mounted is parody. In this extended Bakhtinian view, then, parody is both a symptom and a weapon in the battle between popular cultural energies and the forces of authority which seek to control them.

We must ask, despite the geniality of this whole line of argument, how far it can actually be sustained. As we shall see, the answer is: only partially. Many of the particular accounts that Bakhtin gives, especially of medieval sacred parody and some Early Modern forms, do not bear up under careful scholarly scrutiny (see Chapter 2). Despite these reservations, there is an evident force to this general position with respect to parody, to be recognised as much in the parodic practices of the contemporary world as in the conditions of Early Modern Europe which are Bakhtin's home ground. The extreme relativisation of all languages – the refusal to grant final authority to any one way of speaking over another – which is a characteristic of contemporary popular culture, is evidenced in the pervasiveness of parody, and is testimony to its effect in dissolving the fixed supports of linguistic and cultural authority.

Evidence of this dissolvent effect can be found in the suspicion with which the culturally conservative have viewed parody. In addition to those who view parody as parasitic, and as essentially a minor form, there are those who, while recognising the pleasure and even the critical edge of the mode, wish to restrict it within very narrow bounds. One such is Arthur Quiller-Couch, who provides the preface to a typical early twentieth-century collection of parodic verse, *Parodies and Imitations Old and New* (1912):

> Now, the first thing to be said about Parody is that it plays with the gods: its fun is taken with Poetry, which all good men admit to be a beautiful and adorable thing, and some would have to be a holy thing. It follows then that Parody must be delicate ground, off which the profane and vulgar should be carefully warned. A deeply religious man may indulge a smile at this or that in his religion; as a truly devout lover may rally his mistress on her foibles, since for him they make her the more enchanting ... So, or almost so, should it be with the parodist. He must be friends with the gods, and worthy of their company, before taking these pleasant liberties with them.
>
> (Adam and White, 1912: vi)

This judgement emerges from great confidence and familiarity with the literary tradition to which it considers parody to be addressed. It is interesting, therefore, that it should betray such anxiety about the proper limits of parody, which is in danger, it seems, of becoming a kind of profanity. It must be restricted within very narrow limits, where its desacralising energies will not be allowed out of control. Properly restricted in this way, its pleasures – light and pleasant ones – can be duly enjoyed.

Quiller-Couch, then, acknowledges the potentially subversive action of parody only to deprecate it. This suggests something of

the political (or more widely social) ambivalence of the relativisation of languages propelled by the mode. However, as I have inti-
mated, there is a strong alternative tradition which stresses the
culturally conservative character of parody – which claims that
parody acts, not to increase the relativisation of language, but to
diminish it. It is not difficult to see why this should be so. If
nineteenth-century literary parodies, from *Rejected Addresses*
onwards, are taken as a model, rather than Rabelais or 'The
Comic Strip', then the possibilities for cultural conservatism in
the form become apparent (*Rejected Addresses* was a series of parodies of contemporary writers published in 1812 by two brothers
James and Horace Smith; 'The Comic Strip' was a series of television parodies in the 1980s and 1990s, spoofing such forms as the
self-important Hollywood drama and Enid Blyton adventure stories). Indeed, from this perspective, the anxieties of a writer like
Quiller-Couch seem wholly misplaced. What these literary parodies provide is a series of in-jokes, policing the boundaries of the
sayable, and preserving a notion of the decorous or the 'natural'
by which the absurdities and extremities of writing can be measured. This position is stated (in terms which are perhaps
extreme) by George Kitchin in his 1931 *A Survey of Burlesque and
Parody in English*:

> Parody in modern times, that is since the Seventeenth Century, repre-
> sents the reaction of custom to attempted change, of complacency to
> the adventure of the mind or senses, and of the established political
> or social forces to subversive ideas. Perhaps its character is most
> compendiously summed up by saying that it has for the last three
> centuries been inveterately social and anti-romantic. Politically it has
> tended to become more and more the watchdog of national interests,
> socially of respectability, and, in the world of letters, of established
> forms.

> (Kitchin, 1931: xiii)

You should not be misled by the apparently hostile reference to 'complacency' in this quotation – Kitchin is militantly sympathetic to the conservative function of parody, believing that it serves an hygienic function in cleansing the literary world of those unhealthy tendencies, political and cultural, which periodically threaten to engulf it. Kitchin enthusiastically enunciates, then, one version of the politics of parody – that it has a critically conservative function in defending the common-sense values of 'centrally minded' people against the dangerous extremes that enthusiastic poets are ever likely to fall into.

An example of parody that works in this way comes from the practice of *The Anti-Jacobin*, a journal founded at the end of the eighteenth century to combat sympathy for the principles of the French Revolution. Its contributors, who included George Canning, William Gifford, and John Hookham Frere, relied heavily on parody to assault the new poetics of writers such as William Wordsworth, Samuel Taylor Coleridge and Robert Southey. In the 1790s these writers were all sympathetic to revolutionary sentiments, and were writing poetry of a kind construed by the Tories of *The Anti-Jacobin* as supporting those sympathies. Here for example is what Canning and Frere make of Southey in the 1790s, when he was still sympathetic to the Revolution and before his about-face and embrace of Toryism. The poem is called an 'Inscription; for the Door of the Cell in Newgate where Mrs. Brownrigg, the 'Prentice-cide, was confined previous to her Execution':

> For one long term, or e'er her trial came,
> Here Brownrigg linger'd. Often have these cells
> Echoed her blasphemies, as with shrill voice
> She scream'd for fresh Geneva. Not to her
> Did the blithe fields of Tothill, or thy street,
> St. Giles, its fair varieties expand;
> Till at the last, in slow-drawn cart she went

To execution. Dost thou ask her crime?
SHE WHIPP'D TWO FEMALE 'PRENTICES TO DEATH,
AND HID THEM IN THE COAL-HOLE. For her mind
Shap'd strictest plans of discipline. Sage schemes!
Such as Lycurgus taught, when at the shrine
Of the Orthyan Goddess he bade flog
The little Spartans; such as erst chastised
Our MILTON, when at college. For this act
Did BROWNRIGG swing. Harsh laws! But time shall come
When France shall reign, and laws be all repealed!

                                 (Jerrold and Leonard, 1913: 93)

This splendidly skewers the pomposities of Southey's verse, with its exclamations, its would-be grand diction, its display of learning, and its invocation of the calendar of republican saints ('Our MILTON'). But these stylistic mannerisms are really beside the point, which for Canning and Frere is overwhelmingly a political one – Southey's supposed sympathy for crime, his admiration for revolutionary France, and his adoption of principles that would lead to anarchy. The practice of *The Anti-Jacobin* represents perhaps the most visible example in English literary history of the conservative function of parody.

Is it possible in any way to reconcile these two generally opposed descriptions of parody? i.e., that it is broadly subversive of authority, acting to relativise all official or sacred languages, or that it is broadly conservative in the way that it constantly monitors and ridicules the formally innovative. The answer to this is surely no, if by reconciliation one means any attempt to give an essentialising definition which grants parody a single social or political direction. Parody can do all of the things that these opposed traditions describe; it can subvert the accents of authority *and* police the boundaries of the sayable; it can place all writing under erasure *and* draw a circle around initiated readers to exclude ignorant ones; it can discredit the authority of what has always been said *and* ridicule the new and the formally innovative. We have to recognise, in other words, that parody's direction of attack cannot be decided upon in abstraction from the particular social and historical circumstances in which the parodic act is performed, and therefore that no single social or political meaning can be attached to it. In this respect, the question of the cultural politics of parody is comparable to that of the cultural politics of laughter, which has likewise been claimed both for anti-authoritarian irreverence and as a means of ridiculing and stigmatising the socially marginal and the oppressed.

We can therefore return to the question of the historicity of parody, recognising that if parody is a general feature of discursive situations, the manner in which one can give a particularised historical account of it will have to be recast. It is not that parody, as a discursive mode, has only had one predominant function in the history of cultural forms; rather, we have to describe the ways in which it works at particular historical moments, and to consider the functions it performs in differing social situations. Parody itself is socially and politically multivalent; its particular uses are never neutral, but they cannot be deduced in advance. We can nevertheless recognise that there are particular social and historical situations in which parody is especially likely to flourish, or at least to become the medium of important cultural statements. What are the contours of these situations?

I have already asked whether parody is more likely to flourish in closed social situations (monasteries, etc.) or open ones. Since we have many parodic works which come from both such situations, we must conclude, not that there is no relation between literary modes and social situation, but that the nature of that relationship needs to be specified. In subsequent chapters I will consider some of these parodic forms in more detail: the medieval *parodia sacra*, as well as the parodic practices of ancient Greeks and modern novelists and playwrights. For now we can simply recognise that parody will play very different roles in these differing situations, perhaps reinforcing community norms in a monastery or private boarding school, and being interpretable as an act of piety in both, while at the same time serving to overturn and discredit the discourses of authority in the Early Modern world of Rabelais and Shakespeare.

If it is possible to draw a broad distinction between 'open' and 'closed' societies or social situations, it is perhaps also possible to distinguish between societies characterised by cultural self-confidence or, alternatively, a sense of cultural belatedness. Is parody likely to flourish, that is, in societies like early Modern Europe, or our contemporary 'postmodern' world, in both of which there is a strong sense of a powerful preceding culture? In the former case, which we also know as the 'Renaissance', European culture was suffused with a sense of the great inheritance of classical writing; in our own case, as the various 'post-' coinages suggest, there is a pervasive consciousness of a past which is still strongly present, though the value of that inheritance is deeply contested. Certainly a related form, 'imitation', is widespread in sixteenth- and seventeenth-century writing; in this form, a revered classical model is imitated and updated, and thus given a particular contemporary force. If this is one of the principal forms in which a belated culture manages its relationship to its cultural predecessors, it can be contrasted to the contemporary world, where a more polemical relation to the cultural past often expresses itself in the practice of 'writing back': the canonic texts of the past are scrutinised, challenged, and parodied in the name of the subject positions (of class, race or gender) which they are seen to exclude. In both these periods, then, parody and its related forms are widespread, though the particular polemical direction that these forms adopt differs widely.

A strong contrast can be drawn, here, with the nineteenth century, which, though certainly conscious of its cultural predecessors, was not overwhelmed by this consciousness. In terms of its own cultural production, the nineteenth century saw striking and self-confident achievements in the novel and poetry where, with some exceptions, parody is not central. Nevertheless, this is the period characterised by one anthologist and theorist of parody, Dwight Macdonald, as the 'Golden Age' of parody, a description justified by that tradition of literary parody to which I have alluded, which begins with *The Anti-Jacobin* and *Rejected Addresses*, and culminates in Beerbohm's *A Christmas Garland* (1912). However, we have to recognise the particular ways in which the polemical direction of parody operates in this period. In considering the nineteenth-century novel, for example (a consideration conducted at greater length in Chapter 3), we can recognise the importance of parody to certain novelists: Thackeray above all, but also, to a lesser degree, Jane Austen and George Eliot. For these writers, parody of certain stigmatised modes (the Gothic, or Newgate, silver-fork or sensation novels) acts as a kind of guarantee of their own realist credentials. As for that tradition of literary parody, for the most part it surely justifies that suspicion of parody as an essentially parasitic mode – a bearer of 'pleasant liberties', in Quiller-Couch's phrase – whose polemical direction remains to be specified but which does not fundamentally enter into the creative energies of any of the major writers of the period. So, with the possible exception of Thackeray, the nineteenth century, while being the Golden Age of a certain kind of parody, is not a period in which the mode contributes to any of its major cultural achievements.

Open/closed, belated/self-confident – these are ways of describing whole societies, without paying close attention to the social divisions within them. But these internal divisions too are important (perhaps the most important) in assessing whether a particular social situation is likely to produce parody, and have implications for the kind of parody that is produced. Strongly stratified societies, for example, where separate classes live in relative social isolation, are very likely to produce mutual parodic characterisations of the social layers, whose manners of speech and writing are very strongly marked by class. This is very strikingly the case, for example, in English society, between, roughly, the 1880s and the 1950s. This society was highly socially zoned, and its different groups lived in remarkable ignorance of each other. It was also highly unequal, not only in material terms, but also in terms of access to cultural resources. Unsurprisingly, parody was pervasive, both formally and informally. Mutual mockery of habits of speech indicates one aspect of the pervasiveness of the mode at the informal level; more formally, the institutions of popular culture such as the Music Hall thrived on the parodic recycling of prestigious cultural material, while there was a specific genre of burlesque melodrama within the popular theatre. In an autobiographical account of life in a working-class area at the beginning of the twentieth century, Robert Roberts described how new popular songs were quickly assimilated by the boys of his part of Salford, above all by parody; indeed, parody was one of the principal cultural forms used by working-class people, so much so that people would know the parodic version of sentimental songs or recitations, without knowing the originals. This tradition of working-class parody persisted into Second World War army songs, when ribald versions of classic songs such as 'The Ash Grove' and 'The Minstrel Boy' were widespread; popular entertainment carried forward this genre also, as in such radio and television shows as *ITMA* and *The Goon Show*. When Tommy Cooper or Morecambe and Wise parodied Shakespeare in their acts they were the direct inheritors of this tradition.[1]

We can thus say that there *are* social situations or historical moments when parody is likely to flourish, and to become the medium of important cultural statements. The particular forms that parody takes in such periods, however, remain to be specified, and in general terms we can conclude, unsurprisingly, that the predominant uses of the parodic mode will vary according to the kind of social situation in which it is put to use. In the following chapters the uses of parody will be considered in various social and cultural situations, and in various genres, through to the present day, recognising that its polemical direction, and consequences for the reader's experience, vary widely.

PARODY AS CRITICISM

Before turning to these more substantial accounts of parodies, it is worth considering one final function that parody can serve, namely its capacity to act as criticism. One of the typical ways in which parody works is to seize on particular aspects of a manner or a style and exaggerate it to ludicrous effect. There is an evident critical function in this, as the act of parody must first involve identifying a characteristic stylistic habit or mannerism and then making it comically visible. Take the following example from a 1912 parody by the supreme English literary parodist, Max Beerbohm, called 'The Mote in the Middle Distance':

> It was with the sense of a, for him, very memorable something that he peered now into the immediate future, and tried, not without compunction, to take that period up where he had, prospectively, left it. But just where the deuce *had* he left it? The consciousness of dubiety was, for our friend, not, this morning, quite yet clean-cut enough to outline the figure on what she had called his 'horizon', between which and himself the twilight was indeed of a quality somewhat intimidating.
>
> (Beerbohm, 1993: 3)

Beerbohm attributes this to H*nry J*m*s, and you may well have recognised some of the characteristics of the latter's late style beautifully parodied here: the complicated syntax, the conclusions to sentences endlessly postponed, the shift between the colloquial and the circumlocutory, the metaphor extended to breaking point. The parody draws attention to extreme features of J*m*s's style here, and it therefore acts, in part, in a critical sense.

This critical function has been seized upon as the basis for

some wider claims made on behalf of parody. These claims reproduce, however, the dispute about the cultural politics of parody
that I set out in the previous section. For some writers, parody
serves a normative critical function, indeed, it acts to do so when
the more modern forms of criticism such as the literary essay are
absent, and its function is to make explicit the absurdities of current poetic fashions. On the other hand, it has been claimed,
especially by the group of critics known as Russian Formalists,
that parody can contribute to the evolution of literary style.
Especially in periods of considerable stylistic contention, parody
is one of the weapons wielded on behalf of the new against the
old. And what period is not marked by such contentions? The
battle of the Ancients and the Moderns is being fought at most
moments in literary history. However, the Formalist understanding of literary evolution was not a matter of simple generational
succession; rather, they understood the literary situation in any
period to be a complex system with its elements disposed in particular ways; parody could serve the function of reordering the
elements in the system, allowing previously low-status elements
to take on high-status positions. This process was memorably
described by Viktor Shklovsky as 'the canonisation of the junior
branch'.[2]

   English poetic history is certainly marked by skirmishes which
lend support to both these ways of understanding the critical
function of parody. The battles over style at the end of the eighteenth century and the beginning of the nineteenth century produced, unsurprisingly, a wealth of parodies; Wordsworth, Coleridge
and Southey must be the most parodied poets in the English literary tradition. We have already observed that behind many of these
parodies lurked scarcely concealed political purposes. This is true
of the second generation of Romantic poets also, though the politics were directed in the opposite direction. Percy Bysshe Shelley
marked his distance from the older poet, Wordsworth, in the parody 'Peter Bell the Third', where the complaint is that

Wordsworth has sold out to political reaction and lost sight of his originating poetic impulse:

> Even the Reviewers who were hired
> To do the work of his reviewing,
> With adamantine nerves, grew tired; –
> Gaping and torpid they retired,
> To dream of what they should be doing.
>
> And worse and worse the drowsy curse
> Yawned in him till it grew a pest –
> A wide contagious atmosphere,
> Creeping like cold through all things near;
> A power to infect and to infest.
>
> His servant-maids and dogs grew dull;
> His kitten, late a sportive elf;
> The woods and lakes so beautiful,
> Of dim stupidity were full.
> All grew as dull as Peter's self.
>
> (Jerrold and Leonard, 1913: 206)

The polemical function of parody here is directed to a whole manner or style, that of the late Wordsworth, and looks back to an earlier, more authentic poetry, more genuinely permitting the evolution of a new manner. Parody, in these skirmishes in the culture wars of the beginning of the nineteenth century, is one of the weapons in the struggle over the social and political direction of poetry.

Parody can indeed become the vehicle for a critique of a whole aesthetic, and the substitution of another in its place, as in the following pair of poems. First W.B. Yeats's famous poem from the 1890s, 'The Lake Isle of Innisfree':

> I will arise and go now, and go to Innisfree,
> And a small cabin build there, of clay and wattles made:
> Nine bean-rows will I have there, a hive for the honey-bee,

And live alone in the bee-loud glade.

And I shall have some peace there, for peace comes dropping
　　　slow,
Dropping from the vales of the morning to where the cricket
　　　sings;
There midnight's all a glimmer, and noon a purple glow,
And evening full of the linnet's wings.

I will arise and go now, for always night and day
I hear lake water lapping with low sounds by the shore;
While I stand on the roadway, or on the pavements grey,
I hear it in the deep heart's core.

Now compare the following poem by Ezra Pound, from 1917, called 'The Lake Isle':

O God, O Venus, O Mercury, patron of thieves,
Give me in due time, I beseech you, a little tobacco-shop.
With the little bright boxes
　　　piled up neatly upon the shelves
And the loose fragrant cavendish
　　　and the shag,
And the bright Virginia
　　　loose under the bright glass cases,
And a pair of scales not too greasy,
And the whores dropping in for a word or two in passing,
For a flip word, and to tidy their hair a bit.

O God, O Venus, O Mercury, patron of thieves,
Lend me a little tobacco-shop,
　　　or install me in any profession
Save this damn'd profession of writing
　　　where one needs one's brains all the time.

The immediate polemical target here is not really the idiosyncracies of Yeats's style; indeed, it is quite likely that no reader would recognise this as a parody if it were not for the title. What Pound is attacking, by means of the parody, is a whole aesthetic, a characteristic way of writing and understanding art and its purposes. He attacks a particular vein of late nineteenth-century Romanticism, which combines lyric beauty, plangent melancholy, and fantasies about rural life. Pound's parody gleefully asserts a quite different aesthetic, in which the rituals of urban life, sharply and brightly realised, are offered instead, and where poetry would not come from the 'deep heart's core', but be a product of the intelligence. Poetry, instead of being about the kind of topic that Yeats adopts, and being written in his style, should rather be about *this* matter, and written in *this* manner.

Pound's parody, written at the beginning of the twentieth century, is part of a battle over the direction that poetry should take; crudely, he is repudiating the generic inheritance of Romanticism in favour of the sharper and harder aesthetic we have come to know as Modernism. Where Gifford and Frere had attacked the early Romantics, and Shelley had attacked Wordsworth, so Pound was now taking on Yeats, in battles that all involved the critical repudiation of a style, seen as symptomatic of wider aesthetic and cultural issues.

A further point needs to be made in this context, that parody has the paradoxical effect of preserving the very text that it seeks to destroy, even if the hypotext remains only 'under erasure' (to revert to the vocabulary of Jacques Derrida alluded to on p.15 above). This can have some odd effects, even running counter to the apparent intentions of the parodist. Thus the classic parody of *Don Quixote* (discussed more fully in the next chapter) preserves the very chivalric romances that it attacks – with the unexpected result that for much of its history the novel has been read as a celebration of misplaced idealism rather than a satire of it. In the following chapters I shall have frequent cause to refer to this 'parodic paradox' – understood as the generation of further writing out of the assault upon stigmatised forms that the parody is supposed to bring to a halt. Parody can act to preserve the very forms that it attacks.

I have defined parody, in a deliberately widely drawn definition, as any cultural practice which makes a relatively polemical allusive imitation of another cultural production or practice. The point of this definition was to situate parody in the to-and-fro of language, and to suggest a similarity between the everyday rejoinders of speech and the competitive relations between texts. This is a definition based upon the function of parody in the continuance of human discourse, not upon the formal means by which parody is achieved. Tight definitions of a formal kind can be attempted, but they have the disadvantage of having to deal with large numbers of incompatible definitions and differing national usages. In my account, parody is to be thought of as a mode, or as a range in the spectrum of possible intertextual relations. The specific means by which the polemical purposes of parody are achieved need to be described locally.

It follows from this that the functions which parody serves can vary widely, so that it is impossible to specify any single social or cultural direction for the mode. In fact, the social and cultural meanings of parody, like all utterances, can only be understood in the density of the interpersonal and intertextual relations in which it intervenes. The following chapters attempt to give accounts of parody which bring out its polemical purposes, in widely varying social and cultural situations.

We should not end on this note of academic solemnity, however; let us remember instead that, among its other characteristics, parody can be irreverent, inconsequential, and even silly. It includes the parodies of schoolchildren ('While shepherds washed their socks by night') as much as the learned fun of their elders (Pope's parody of Chaucer: 'Women ben full of Ragerie,/Yet swinken not sans secresie'). It need not be funny, yet it works better if it is, because laughter, even of derision, helps it secure its point. But sometimes – and this is a consideration which I have certainly not emphasised enough – the laughter is the only point, and the breakdown of discourse into nonsense is a sufficient reward in itself:

> The boy stood on the burning deck,
> His feet were covered with blisters.
> He had no trousers of his own
> And so he wore his sister's.

It is not for nothing that parody is a close cousin, perhaps even a progenitor, of the tradition of English nonsense poetry that descends from the seventeenth century and includes Edward Lear and Lewis Carroll, who were both accomplished parodists. If the following pages should remain too long in solemn regions, please bring to mind the latter's parody of Southey's smug didacticism, and apply the lesson accordingly:

> 'You are old,' said the youth, 'and your jaws are too weak
> For anything other than suet;
> Yet you finished the goose, with the bones and the beak –
> Pray, how did you manage to do it?'

> 'In my youth,' said his father, 'I took to the law,
> And argued each case with my wife;
> And the muscular strength which it gave to my jaw,
> Has lasted the rest of my life.'

Nevertheless, it is clear that ancient Greek culture was shot through with parodic forms, even if their relationship to the heroic, tragic or sacred texts is difficult to determine. Thus one of the primary meanings of the Greek *parodia* was the recognised form of the poem written in epic Homeric style but with a trivial or 'low' topic – the *Batrachomyomachia* is the only surviving example. The great tragic trilogies, such as Aeschylus' *Oresteia*, were in fact always performed as tetralogies, of which the fourth was a satyr play, with at least a partially parodic relationship to the serious matter which preceded it. 'Burlesque of legend', to use a phrase of the critic Gilbert Norwood, was one of the staples of Greek comedy (Norwood, 1964: 23). These examples are all taken from the great moment of Athenian democracy in the fifth century BCE; but we can also trace a tradition of serio-comic writing through Hellenic and then Roman culture in which parody plays a central role. In the previous chapter it was noted that the first recorded usage of the word parody occurs in Aristotle; this derivation of the word from the ancient Greek suggests as much the prevalence of the practice in Greek culture as the authority of the great philosopher.

The widest context for this profusion of parodic forms is the contested status of the stories about the Olympian Gods, since it is the often scandalous incidents of these legends which provide the opportunity for parody, as Norwood notes. Homer, as the great source and repository of many of these stories, provides both the stylistic model and the narrative opportunity for parodies of all kinds. Both mock-heroic (high style, low topic) and travesty (high topic, low style) can be found in relation to the great epic poet. What remains extraordinarily difficult to establish is the effect of this parody on the sacred stories themselves. Part of the difficulty concerns the very status of religious myth in classical Greece, where religion was unsupported by a priestly caste, bound in with the ritual life of the people, and the occasion for Dionysian as well as civic celebration. It thus had a status quite unlike that of Christianity, and the categories of the modern (i.e.

post-medieval) world simply do not translate to this early social world. It is not therefore useful to speak of popular and elite culture, or even of the carnivalesque, though perhaps some of the Dionysiac celebrations had a comparable role to medieval and Renaissance carnival. At all events, the Greeks seemed able to sustain an attitude or frame of mind in which the serious forms and their parodic counterparts could exist side by side, even when these serious forms – and thus their parodies – carried some of the most sacred stories of their culture.

Parody also presents peculiar difficulties for translators, especially general parody where the translator has to find some equivalent in the target language of the mode which is parodied in the source text. But this difficulty points to a wider one, in that the very understanding of ancient Greek parody has necessarily been filtered through the particular cultural situations of those who have tried to make sense of it. Thus the *Batrachomyomachia*, or the *Battle of the Frogs and Mice*, is widely described as mock-heroic (I have just done so myself); the poem certainly treats the affairs of frogs and mice in high Homeric style. However, to describe the poem in this way inevitably translates it into the cultural situation of seventeenth- and eighteenth-century mock-heroic; it is not for nothing that one of the principal translations of the poem in English is by Thomas Parnell in 1717, aided in part by his friend Alexander Pope. At all events, here is an example of Parnell's translation, taken from the second Book when the mice, inspired by their King, advance in martial array upon the frogs:

> His Words in ev'ry breast inspir'd Alarms,
> And careful *Mars* supply'd their Host with Arms.
> In verdant Hulls despoil'd of all their Beans,
> The buskin'd Warriours stalk'd along the Plains,
> Quills aptly bound, their bracing Corselet made,
> Fac'd with the Plunder of a Cat they flay'd,
> The lamp's round Boss affords their ample Shield;

> Large Shells of Nuts their cov'ring helmet yield;
> And o'er the Region, with reflected Rays,
> Tall Groves of Needles for their Lances blaze.
> Dreadful in Arms the marching Mice appear.[1]

This has clearly been filtered through a sensibility which has read Garth's *Dispensary* and *The Rape of the Lock* – neoclassical mock-heroic poems which I discuss in Chapter 4. Nevertheless, we can recognise here a typical parodic moment, in which the manner and style of heroic poetry is adapted for comic purposes to trivial matters. This style of writing is unequivocally known as *parodia* in Greek discussion.

If this manner appears mock-heroic to a modern sensibility because it deals with low matter in an elevated style, then it is also true that the opposite effect is readily found in Greek culture, notably in the satyr plays, which typically travesty the high material handled with such dignity in the tragedies that precede them. Even here, however, it is difficult to be certain, since only Euripides' *Cyclops* survives, and it is not even certain which tragic trilogy it originally accompanied – nor is it certain which of the various other fragments went with which tragic originals. But it is probable that satyr plays did not provide specific parody of the preceding material; rather, they characteristically presented, in the words of Dana Sutton, 'a famous mythological character in a grotesque situation rich in comic possibilities' (Sutton, 1980: 13). Thus *Cyclops* provides a structural parody of the Cyclops episode in the *Odyssey*: Odysseus arrives in Sicily, the home for the purposes of the play of various Cyclops, where he finds Silenus and his troop of satyrs already imprisoned by Polyphemus; he eventually escapes in the prescribed manner (blinding of the Cyclops's one eye with pointed stick), but only after a couple of his men have provided a gorily described meal for his host. Certainly Polyphemus's man-eating appetites and his drinking provide some opportunity for what Bakhtin describes as 'grotesque realism', which is juxtaposed to the self-serving grandiloquence of Odysseus; and the presence of the comically appetitive and cowardly Silenus and his chorus of satyrs (costumed with horse tails and giant *phalloi*) ensures that we are recognisably in a comic and not a heroic world. But it is difficult to see exactly how far the heroic story is being attacked, or what damage such a play might do to the elevation of either tragedy or the heroic tradition; the Greeks seemed to be able to inhabit both worlds simultaneously, and however reductive the notion of 'comic relief', it is hard to avoid it altogether.

As far as can be determined, then, satyr plays were a travestying form which presented heroic and more generally mythological legends in a reductively comic way. They did not contain specific parody, but relied more upon structural parody, though given the fragmentary nature of the evidence, the precise nature of this is impossible to establish.[2] Old Comedy, however (the name by which the comedy of the late fifth century BCE is known, including most of the plays of Aristophanes), certainly did contain much specific parody. This is a much more secular form than the satyr play, directly contemporary and political in the hands of Aristophanes, but also containing much 'burlesque of legend'. Aristophanes' plays themselves are full of parodic allusions, most notably to the plays of Euripides; but his comedy is truly a heteroglossic (multi-languaged) form, made up of the multiple voices that competed with each other in the bustling civic life of ancient Athens. Again this poses acute problems for the translator; this is how one modern version of the play *Thesmophoriazûsae* (sometimes translated as *The Poet and the Women*) is prefaced by its writer:

> The *disjecta membrae* of Shakspere, the Border Ballads, popular tear-jerkers, and badly remembered passages from various devotional works, are far from being thoughtless or accidental; they are one way of suggesting the hundreds of quotations, misquotations, and overt

and hidden allusions with which Aristophanes has salted this extraordinary poem.

(Fitts, 1962: 257)

Other translators have made similar choices, trying to find contemporary equivalents for the specific parodies with which the plays of Aristophanes abound; the context for these particular imitations, however, is a much wider practice of allusion, the full texture of which is now irrecoverable.

However, these old comedies do abound with specific parodies, of Euripides in *The Acharnians*, of Socrates and the Sophists in *The Clouds*, of Bellerophon in *The Peace*, of Agathon and Euripides in *Thesmophoriazûsae*, and of Aeschylus and Euripides again in *The Frogs*. This last play includes a dramatic contest between Aeschylus and Euripides in the underworld, with each trying to undermine the other's style of play-writing; this is a situation designed to provide the opportunity for parody, as in this version of Euripides in the lyric mode:

> Sea birds
> Over the wavetops wheeling, chattering,
> > Wee birds!
> Wing tips dip,
> Splashing in the –
> Plashing in the –
> See how their feathers glisten in the sea-spray –
>
> > Spiders
> Up in the rafters, underneath the ceiling
> > Why does
> Each little foot go
> Twiddling and
> Twiddling and –
> Busy little weavers working at the loom!
>
> (Aristophanes, 1964: 203–4)

In the fiction of the play, this parody is actually written by Aeschylus as a parody of the style of his younger rival; one way of interpreting *The Frogs* has thus been to see it as an assault on the 'modern' style of play-writing which Euripides is presumed to represent. Certainly in this version, the translator has worked hard to provide a modern equivalent of the stylistic features of Euripides parodied in the original, complete with comic rhymes ('spiders' … 'why does') and foolish diction ('plashing' and 'twiddling'). But it remains uncertain just how seriously the assault upon Euripides is to be taken; given the fragmentary survival of this material (now two and a half thousand years old), any attempt to deduce fully worked out socio-cultural attitudes from the evidence must be largely conjectural.

Old Comedy, then – or at least the plays of Aristophanes – is a form which is marked by parodic forms on at least two levels. First, the very texture of the plays is made up of myriad allusions to the contemporary language of Athens; second, the plays abound with specific parodies of tragic (and other) writers, the cultural politics of which is now hard to determine. But as with the satyr plays, it is probably safer to conclude that the genres (tragedy and comedy) are in coexistence, rather than in competition with each other. At all events, fifth-century Athens displayed an extraordinary tolerance and enjoyment of parody, which both seized upon the serious genres and permitted them to coexist.

It is also possible to trace the presence of parody in the writings of Plato, produced in the fourth century. The potential for parody in the Socratic dialogue is apparent, since the form characteristically involves Socrates's interlocutors setting out their case before it is shredded by their interrogator. Again we need to make the usual caveat: the exact nature of the parody is often difficult to determine given that the texts of Socrates's opponents have usually not survived. But it is useful to recognise that parody is a formal possibility in Plato's writings, since its presence indicates the profoundly serio-comic aspect of his writing, which will serve as an important model for later writing, both Greek and Roman. This characteristic can be seen most clearly in *The Symposium*, an account of a drinking party in which the various guests compete to give the best speech about the nature of love. Several of those present speak before Socrates's turn; in the words of a modern translator, most of these 'are probably parodies of their supposed speakers' (Hamilton, 1951: 12). Thus Agathon (a playwright, all of whose plays have been lost) is given a speech in the best rhetorical manner of the sophists, a persistent target of Plato's; it concludes with the following splendid peroration or climax:

> It is Love who empties us of the spirit of estrangement and fills us with the spirit of kinship; who makes possible such mutual inter-course as this; who presides over festivals, dances, sacrifices; who bestows good-humour and banishes surliness; whose gift is the gift of good-will and never of ill-will. He is easily entreated and of great kindness; contemplated by the wise, admired by the gods; coveted by men who possess him not, the treasure of those who are blessed by his possession; father of Daintiness, Delicacy, Voluptuousness, all Graces, longing and desire; careful of the happiness of good men, careless of the fate of bad; in toil, in fear, in desire, in speech the best pilot, soldier, comrade, saviour; author of order in heaven and earth; loveliest and best of all leaders of song, whom it behoves every man to follow singing his praise, and bearing his part in that melody wherewith he casts a spell over the minds of all gods and all men.
>
> (Plato, 1951: 71–2)

If you were enraptured by this, you might wish to resist the idea that it is parody; but it certainly is, and within a few sentences of the conclusion of Agathon's speech, Socrates has reduced the speaker to a humiliating admission that he does not know what he is talking about. The parody here is of a rhetorical style which relies upon fine-sounding words and their elegant arrangement, rather than upon painstaking inquiry into the truth; we do not have to subscribe to this particular view of rhetoric to recognise that the results of a certain kind of rhetorical training are being parodied. Again, the effect in English is dependent upon the translation; here, the translator has done well to reproduce the carefully climactic series of clauses, many of them repeating the same antithetical structure. Parody is being deployed in this instance as a way of establishing the superiority of the Socratic method, which carefully avoids all such verbal artfulness in favour of a more inquisitorial pursuit of the truth.

Plato is one possible ancestor for (and also one frequent target in) a tradition of serio-comic writing which is heavily dependent upon parody, and which continued through the Hellenistic and Roman worlds and into the Christian era. This tradition has come to be known as the 'menippea' or 'menippean satire', after the Greek writer Menippus, whose work was widely imitated but which only survives in fragments. The fullest contemporary account of the genre is by Joel C. Relihan, *Ancient Menippean Satire* (1993), in which the author makes plain the centrality of parody in it. Menippean satire, by this generic description, is characterised by more than the presence of prose and poetry and of a serio-comic attitude, though these are important if relatively superficial generic markers. More fundamentally in this account the genre provided a learned parody of learning, or indeed a philosophical parody of philosophy, by means of a comic self-parodying narrator. Examples of the genre, apart from the lost works of Menippus and his Latin successor Varro, include Petronius's *Satyricon* and Seneca's *Apocolocyntosis* (both first century AD), through to Boethius's *Consolation of Philosophy* (sixth century). The *Satyricon*, which mixes poetry and prose, gaiety and obscenity, learning and the satire of learning, demonstrates the parodic self-defeating nature of the genre with particular clarity, for its hero Encolpius is both the reader's guide through a series of comic, obscene and satirical adventures, and himself the greediest and most salacious of the characters. The work contains incidental parody, switches between prose and poetry in ways which are at times serious and at other times comically reductive, and generally deploys its imitative skills in ways which require the reader to be alert to all the varying tones which the parodic forms can encompass. The central surviving episode, a dinner at Trimalchio's, is a parody of the platonic Symposium, where the learning of the ancient Greek speakers is replaced by displays of ignorance, stupidity and luxurious vulgarity.

Roughly contemporary is Seneca's *Apocolocyntosis*, written shortly after the death of the Emperor Claudius, and consisting of an account of his failed attempt at an apotheosis (deification) and his descent into Hell as a result. The mixture of prose and poetry permits much incidental parody, as in this version of epic grandiloquence:

> Now Phoebus had made short the arc of day,
> Shortening his road, and Sleep extends its sway;
> Now vaster realms hear Cynthia's conquering call;
> Foul winter plucks the crown from wealthy Fall;
> Bacchus is told, Grow old; no vine escapes,
> As the tardy vintner plucks the few last grapes.
>
> (Seneca, 1977: 221)

In a manner typical of the reductiveness of the genre, this piece of sounding nonsense is immediately followed by this comment in prose: 'I think it'll be better understood if I put it this way: it was the month of October, the thirteenth day of October'. The genre provides many opportunities for this kind of demystifying parody; in the case of the *Apocolocyntosis*, a more general assault upon the recently deceased Claudius is conducted by means of a parody of the council of the Gods, and another of the judgement in Hell. In the former, for example, Hercules is chosen as Claudius's advocate, because of a long tradition in which he is renowned for his gluttony – a quality which makes him an appropriate spokesman for the late Emperor.

Menippean satire does not point to any consistent philosophical attitude, except perhaps to a common sense which distrusts any high-falutin' or long-winded ways of claiming to understand or make sense of the world. In the cognate writings of the second-century AD Hellenistic writer Lucian, parody also plays a central role. However, the cultural situation of a Greek writer five hundred years after Aristophanes or Plato was very different from his Athenian forebears. Lucian was writing in a period known as the Second Sophistic, a period of conscious revival of Greek culture, where the practice of *mimesis* or imitation of great literary predecessors formed a staple of education. Parody here becomes almost a manner of learning; certainly this was a period which was very conscious of its belatedness in relation to a past golden age. Parody plays a central role in Lucian's writing; *The Judging of the Goddesses*, for example, is a comic prose version of the story of the judgement of Paris, while *The Assembly of the Gods* gives the same treatment to a council of the Gods, much as Seneca had done, where the topic is the willingness to admit into Olympus too many human aliens – perhaps alluding to current Roman citizenship laws. Both works are more comic than serious; what is perhaps remarkable is that the old Greek pantheon has survived long enough to give the demystifying spirit of parody some continued leverage.

The works of Lucian, or indeed the works of the other Greek writers that I discussed, did not have a vital presence in medieval culture, though one of the works of the menippean tradition, Boethius's *The Consolation of Philosophy*, was certainly widely known; it was translated into Anglo-Saxon, for example, by Alfred the Great, and into English by Chaucer. However, there was a remarkable range of parodic forms in the medieval period, which included direct liturgical parodies, though the meaning of these forms remain hotly debated. And indeed this was the case in the medieval period itself, where an ambivalence towards parodic forms is evinced by the fact that they were both widely practised and as fiercely condemned. While we cannot describe medieval Christendom as striated by parody in the manner of ancient Greece, we can none the less recognise that, as far as the official Latin culture was concerned, there were a variety of widely circulating written parodic forms.

What perhaps seems most surprising about medieval parodic forms is that they are focused on the most sacred texts of the culture, namely the Bible and the liturgy. A contemporary scholar of medieval Latin parody, Martha Bayless, distinguishes four principal forms: allegorical parody, mock saints' lives, liturgical parodies, and humorous centos (in which lines from the Bible or other classic sources are taken and rearranged to make a new, comic, text). I shall take these forms in turn.

The principal text which can be considered as an allegorical parody is the *Cena Cypriani*, an early medieval piece which was widely copied. It describes the behaviour of a series of guests at a wedding feast given by Joel, king of Cana – wedding guests who include many of the principal figures of the Bible, each with a distinguishing characteristic:

> Adam in the middle, Eve on a leaf
> Cain on a plough, Abel on a milk pail.

The parodic element here is real, but weak; at times this is little more than a didactic text which instructs readers in the Bible by semi-humorous means. Nevertheless, it does surround the sacred stories with a comic atmosphere.

A second medieval form is the mock saint's life, often written about St Nemo (St Nobody) or St Invicem (St One-another). The basic formal impulse here comes from a kind of word-play or grammatical joke, suggesting a scholarly or clerical provenance for the form; in the words of Bayless, 'the texts do prove ... that scholars and clerics were both able and eager to elaborate word-play into sophisticated mock-religious amusements' (Bayless, 1996: 92). Nearer to a potentially desacralising form of writing are the numerous liturgical parodies that are to be found in the medieval period. These parodies typically take the form of Drinkers' masses, in which the words of the liturgy are slightly changed to convert them into masses to the Cask, where Dolio ('cask') appears for Domino ('Lord'), or where *potemus* ('let us drink') is substituted for *oremus* ('let us pray'). Sometimes these are close to, or are indeed, Goliardic verse (kinds of medieval poetry celebrating love and drink). A more doleful and less celebratory version is the gambler's mass, where equivalent transformations turn the words of the liturgy into the cant of gambling. Finally, there is the cento, a new composition created by rearranging lines or passages from a well-known text or texts; the form had its origin in classical antiquity and survived until the seventeenth century. This is the nearest point at which parody begins to break down its hypotext (in this case the Bible) into something like nonsense, or at least, when its textuality becomes the basis for the formal rearrangement required by parody.

Vernacular religious culture (i.e. religious culture in the vernacular languages, not in Latin) also had a strongly parodic element, expressed in rituals that were widespread in the later medieval church. The most famous of these is that of the Feast of Fools, usually held on the feast of the Holy Innocents (December 28), though a range of carnivalesque celebrations occurred during the Christmas season. In a manner directly reminiscent of carnival celebrations, junior clergy performed an elaborate parody of the liturgy, electing a bishop or abbot of fools, wearing their vestments back to front or women's clothes, and performing various other rituals of inversion, such as using old shoes instead of incense in the censor, and braying, hissing, shouting, cackling or jeering the responses. All these rituals were perhaps symbolic of the 'world turned upside down'; they certainly involved some very specific inversions of the religious meanings of medieval Catholicism.[3] In fifteenth-century England, these rituals took the milder form of the election of boy bishops, but even though these ceremonies were generally licensed by the senior clergy, they still involved some parody of the liturgy. These boy-bishop ceremonies, to some extent, and the Feasts of Fools, to a much greater extent, were repeatedly condemned by senior Church authorities; indeed, it is chiefly owing to these condemnations that the practices are known to us. They were effectively repressed either by the Protestant Reformation or by the equally militant Catholic Counter-Reformation. But the late medieval Church could apparently tolerate, albeit with periodical denunciations, parodic practices within and without the buildings of the church in which the authority figures, the rituals, and the sacred words of religion themselves, were all subjected to laughing inversion.

What can be made of these various medieval parodic forms? They have been the subject of wide disagreement as to what they tell us about the status of parody in medieval culture, and indeed about the nature of that culture more generally. On the one hand Bakhtin makes them figure in his various histories of the novel (and especially in his book *Rabelais and His World*, 1984b) as precursors of the novelistic attitude, in which they testify to a humorous ambience surrounding the sacred word and subjecting it to a desacralising attention. In this account, the medieval parodic forms indicate the presence of carnival in medieval culture; their source is ultimately to be traced therefore to popular cultural energies, which permeate official literate culture from the bottom up. When, at the end of the medieval period, there is an explosion of these carnival celebrations, their relativising potential will be seized upon above all by the novel. On the other hand, the obviously clerical provenance of these parodic forms has led other scholars to deny any popular element in them. So Bayless accepts Bakhtin with respect to the pervasiveness of humour (and more widely, carnival) in medieval culture, but rejects what she sees as the Marxist notion that laughter (or carnival) is intrinsically subversive of official hierarchies. She rejects this principally on empirical grounds; all the parodic material that she discusses is written in Latin, implies learned authors and learned readers or listeners, and was produced predominantly by and for monks. In other words, far from parodying the official and sacred, the various traditions of parody that she discusses were produced from the heart of – and at times from near the apex of – the very institution which Bakhtin sees as its principal butt. This argument thus equally contradicts those who have sought to modify Bakhtin's argument on 'safety-valve' lines, that is, that parodic energies, like carnival, provide an outlet for subversive energies which would otherwise be dangerously suppressed; if humour and parody need not be thought of as antipathetic to official culture, then they need not be thought of as *permitted antipathy* either. Similarly, Noel Malcolm in his book *The Origins of English Nonsense* (1997) (discussed in Chapter 4), denies the popular provenance of late sixteenth- and seventeenth-century parody, on the grounds that parody is an intrinsically learned and not a popular mode. These two scholars, then, suggest at the very least an empirical correction to a generally Bakhtinian account of medieval and Early Modern parody, which suggests that it should not be considered subversive of official culture, that its provenance is not to be sought in the popular institution of the carnival but in the learned bastions of that official culture, and that far from being subversive it happily coexisted with the religious forms that it apparently mocked.

It will immediately be recognised that this is a local version of the wider debate about the cultural and political meanings of parody which was discussed in the previous chapter. It is evidently impossible to resolve this question in general terms; that is, it seems more like an act of faith than of scholarship to decide between 'popular energies' or 'monastic laughter' as the origin of medieval *parodia sacra*. However, we can draw upon another aspect of Bakhtinian thought to come at this problem from another way, namely, the insistence that all utterances (including 'cultural' ones) occur in specific situations, and that their mean-

3

PARODY IN THE NOVEL

A ONE-SIDED HISTORY OF THE NOVEL

It would be perfectly possible to write the history of the European novel, at least since *Don Quixote* at the beginning of the seventeenth century, in terms which place a central emphasis upon its use of parody. In such a critical history, the novel establishes itself and its credentials for serious consideration by the deployment of parody, which it uses to devalue alternative genres and their ways of depicting the world. Central to this account, which does exist, though my emphasis on parody (rather than irony) is unusual, is the distinction between the novel and *romance*. This genre has been the butt of parody since Cervantes, though, as we shall see, many other genres have come to take the place of romance as the object of novelistic attack via parody.[1] Romance is above all the genre of wish-fulfilment, ruled by coincidence and wonder – which are other names for the action of Providence. The novel, by contrast, is a more fully secular genre, inhabiting the world as it is and not as it might be, and consistently debunking the claims of romance by making them bump up against the harder, but also more ordinary, facts of existence. Parody is the favoured mode for performing these acts of debunking, carrying out just that polemical function which,

I have argued, defines it; parody therefore enters into the very texture of the novel, defining its relation to other devalued modes and establishing its claims for a more realistic apprehension of human life.

The first half of this chapter consists of a one-sided history of the novel in these terms – what at times I shall refer to as a 'putative' history, for while it is certainly a possible one, its particular emphases may need subsequent correction. I start with a consideration of *Don Quixote*, which is often offered as the 'first' European novel, and given what I have just suggested, certainly deserves to be so considered. The whole point of the novel, one can say, is its attack upon the chivalric romance as a guide to life; the novel repeatedly works by belabouring its romance-obsessed hero, as giants turn out to be windmills, armies turn out to be flocks of sheep, magic helmets barber's basins, and magic potions have a violently emetic effect. This is certainly the view of the novel offered in its 'Prologue', as a (fictional) correspondent of Cervantes is quoted to reassure the professedly modest author about the purpose of the book:

> if I understand it correctly, this book of yours has no need of any of the things you say it lacks, for it is, from beginning to end, an attack upon the books of chivalry, of which Aristotle never dreamed or St. Basil said a word or Cicero had any knowledge ... It has only to avail itself of imitation in its writing, and the more perfect the imitation the better the work will be. And as this piece of yours aims at nothing more than to destroy the authority and influence which books of chivalry have in the world and with the public, there is no need for you to go begging for aphorisms from philosophers, precepts from Holy Scripture, fables from poets, speeches from orators, or miracles from saints, but merely to take care that your sentences flow musically, pleasantly and plainly, with clear, proper, and well-placed words, setting forth your purpose to the best of your power, and putting your ideas intelligibly, without confusion or obscurity.

> (Cervantes, 1981: 13)

above are attributed to Don Quixote himself; they act, in fact, as an indication of his state of mind and even of a whole mentality. Parody of this kind initiates one of its characteristic uses in the novel over the succeeding centuries, where falsifying or repudiated forms (chivalric romance, in this case) are seen as infecting the mentality of the characters. The point of many novels will be to bring such characters to a saner or healthier view of the world; their comedy will spring from the distance between the characters' misrecognition of the world in the light of some false generic ideas, and the everyday actuality which in fact makes it up. Sheep are misrecognised as dauntless knights; laundry boxes will be mistaken for Gothic chests (*Northanger Abbey*); banal provincial seducers will be doted on as heroes of romance (*Madame Bovary*). Cervantes indicates the mentality of his hero in a relatively simple way – Quixote sits on his horse and spouts page after page of direct parody of the chivalric romances which have turned his brain. Later novels will find other formal ways of alluding to the forms which they seek to repudiate, where the parody will operate sometimes in this extended way, but often via passing allusion, turns of phrase, or perhaps extended ironic intimations of their heroes' or heroines' mentalities. But at all events, parodied forms are seen here, and will be in the succeeding history of the novel, as inhabiting the minds of characters, and novels (this is what makes them novels) use parody to expose this delusive mentality to ridicule and correction.

A further point then suggests itself in relation to the function of parody in *Don Quixote* and the succeeding tradition: that it is indeed a weapon in the culture wars of the period. Cervantes' claim in the Prologue, that the novel is 'an attack upon the books of chivalry', is the essential context for understanding his use of parody. The Early Modern period in Spain, perhaps even across Europe, was witness to acute struggles over the values and ideology of the aristo-military caste, of which chivalric romances such as *Amadis of Gaul* and *Palmerin of England*, both parodied in *Don*

Quixote, are prime examples. In later centuries, when different social and cultural battles are being fought, then other forms will be the subject of contention, such as Gothic writing, or bourgeois romance, or the language of advertising. In these contexts, the polemical function of parodic imitation is especially evident.

Finally, we should notice the preferred normative version of style that Cervantes proffers in the Prologue, and which can be used to measure the absurdities and exaggerations of the parodied and repudiated genre. The author stresses the importance of 'imitation' (that is, imitation of 'nature'), so that style itself is a matter of ease, pleasantness and simplicity: 'take care that your sentences flow musically, pleasantly and plainly, with clear, proper, and well-placed words, setting forth your purpose to the best of your power, and putting your ideas intelligibly, without confusion or obscurity.' Cervantes perhaps anticipates here certain typically neoclassical notions of decorum, which emphasise ease and clarity in writing; he will certainly be followed by a tradition of novelistic writing and criticism which justifies its repudiation of other genres by reference to the ease and simplicity, the 'naturalness', with which the novel writes of the world.

Don Quixote, then, provides a prototype for the European novel, in which many of its characteristic features are already apparent. At the very centre of this prototype is the integral use of parody, used often to indicate the delusive mentality of the protagonist or other characters, and as a weapon in the culture wars in which the novel is engaged. 'Novelness' itself, in fact, is partly constituted by the use of parody, for that is the chosen weapon by which the distinctiveness of novel from romance is indicated. How far is this prototype followed in the history of the novel, especially of the novel in English?

If we consider the history of the novel in English in the eighteenth and nineteenth centuries, it is apparent that the answer is: to a very great extent. Taking the work of three English novelists, Henry Fielding, Jane Austen and William Makepeace Thackeray, we can immediately see the centrality of parody within the genre. Fielding's use of parody, at the opening moment of the spectacular rise of the novel in English in the mid-eighteenth century, is absolutely central to his work. He is propelled into novel-writing, indeed, by the desire to parody the work of his contemporary Samuel Richardson, which he did in the short polemical work *Shamela* (1741). This work, which anticipates the parodic work of the more fully novelistic *Joseph Andrews* (1742), is a direct parodic assault upon Richardson's epistolary novel *Pamela* (1740–1). In this latter novel, the heroine is a servant girl who successfully defends her virtue against the lascivious assaults of her master – so successfully, indeed, that he is eventually forced to marry her and thereby to elevate her to his own rank in society. The morality of this, both in class and gender terms, so enraged Fielding that he was provoked into writing first *Shamela* and then *Joseph Andrews*, which parodies Richardson's text by supposing a footman brother to Pamela who comically defends his virtue against the advances of his female employer.

The nature of the parody in *Shamela* is simple enough:

Thursday Night, Twelve o'Clock.

Mrs. Jervis and I are just in bed, and the door unlocked; if my master should come – Odsbobs! I hear him just coming in at the door. You see I write in the present tense, as Parson Williams says. Well, he is in bed between us, we both shamming a sleep; he steals his hand into my bosom, which I, as if in my sleep, press close to me with mine, and then pretend to awake. – I no sooner see him, but I scream out to Mrs. Jervis, she feigns likewise but just to come to herself; we both begin, she to becall, and I to bescratch very liberally. After having made a pretty free use of my fingers, without any great regard to the parts I attack'd, I counterfeit a swoon. Mrs. Jervis then cries out, O sir, what have you done? you have murdered poor Pamela: she is gone, she is gone. –

(Fielding, 1963: 12)

The targets of Fielding's satire are evident here: Richardson's relative explicitness about sexual matters is reinterpreted as prurience, Pamela's innocence is attacked as shamming and hypocrisy, while her defence of her virtue is to be seen as a wholly calculated effort to 'catch' her master. The skill of the parody is to suggest all these things efficiently and comically, with even a glance at the 'immediacy' of Richardson's use of the present tense, permitted by the convention of the epistolary novel.

Shamela is a specific parody, which is expanded into the more general parody of *Joseph Andrews*. If the earlier text simply turned Pamela into Shamela – the innocent into the hypocrite – the novel attacks its target by a process of gender reversal, so that Pamela's brother, Joseph, has to defend his virtue against the salacious advances of his mistress. Joseph, unlike his sister, is a genuine innocent, and some of the comedy of the novel derives from the spectacle of a handsome and vigorous young man innocently rebutting or failing to understand the intentions of a sexually aggressive woman:

> 'I don't intend to turn you away, Joey,' said she, and sighed; 'I am afraid it is not in my power.' She then raised herself a little in her bed, and discovered one of the whitest necks that ever was seen; at which Joseph blushed. 'La!' says she, in an affected surprise, 'what am I doing? I have trusted myself with a man alone, naked in bed; suppose you should have any wicked intentions upon my honour, how should I defend myself?' Joseph protested that he never had the least evil design against her. 'No,' says she, 'perhaps you may not call your designs wicked; and perhaps they are not so.' – He swore they were not.

> (Fielding, 1963: 11)

The scene continues in a similar vein with Joseph obtusely failing to act upon Lady Booby's hints. The novel is more distantly parodic of *Pamela* than *Shamela*, yet is nevertheless close enough for us to recognise that there is a strong polemical impetus, which means that *Joseph Andrews* can be understood as taking its starting-point from the need to differentiate itself from Richardson's novel.

Fielding's activity as a novelist, then, is founded upon his parodic distance from the work of Richardson, which, as far as *Pamela* is concerned, we can describe as providing a kind of bourgeois romance, an eighteenth-century Cinderella story in which the heroine gets to marry her class superior thanks to her aggressive defence of her virtue. Fielding's parodic assault on this tendentious narrative defines his point of departure as a novelist; it can itself be subjected to diverse evaluations. On the one hand, it can be seen as a healthy rejoinder to the narrowness and prurience of Richardson's puritanical ideas of sexual virtue. On the other hand, it is not difficult to see some conservative and normative judgements operating in Fielding's parodies, which mock Pamela's class presumption, and derive their humour from the inherently risible spectacle of a sexually aggressive older woman making advances to an innocent young man. Either way, the presence of parody, in defining the distance of Fielding's novel from the bourgeois romance of Richardson, is sufficiently clear; equally evident is the use of parody in the cultural clashes of the mid-eighteenth century over ethics, class, and sexuality.

Parody is also present in Fielding's later novel, *Tom Jones* (1749), which repeats the soon-to-be canonical formula by which the novel is distinguished from romance: 'truth distinguishes our writing from those idle romances which filled with monsters, the productions, not of nature, but of distempered brains' (Fielding, 1980: 151). Parody is, if anything, more widely present in this later book, where a prevalent note is the pervasiveness of lightly mocked 'high' languages, which are repeatedly made to run up against the 'low' realities of life. These parodied dialects can appear as mock-heroic, or mock-learned, or, as here, as the vocabulary of the traditional lover of romance:

'Oh Sophia,' [Jones is apostrophising his absent mistress] 'would Heaven give thee to my arms, how blest would be my condition! Curst be that fortune which sets a distance between us. Was I but possessed of thee, one only suit of rags thy whole estate, is there a man on earth whom I would envy! How contemptible would the brightest Circassian beauty, drest in all the jewels of the Indies, appear to my eyes! But why do I mention another woman? Could I think my eyes capable of looking at any other woman with tenderness, these hands should tear them from my head. No, my Sophia, if cruel fortune separates us for ever, my soul shall doat on thee alone.'

Jones continues in this vein, until:

At these words he started up, and beheld – not his Sophia – no, nor a Circassian maid richly and elegantly attired for the Grand Signior's seraglio. No; without a gown, in a shift that was somewhat of the coarsest, and none of the cleanest, bedewed likewise with some odoriferous effluvia, the produce of the day's labour, with a pitch-fork in her hand, Molly Seagrim approached ... Here ensued a parley, which, as I do not think myself obliged to relate, I shall omit. It is sufficient that it lasted a full quarter of an hour, at the conclusion of which they retired into the thickest part of the grove.

(Fielding, 1980: 239–40)

Fielding parodies here, clearly enough, the hyperboles of Jones's lover's discourse; when confronted with a far coarser reality in the form of Molly Seagrim, and the simplicity of his own sexual desire, these exaggerations collapse. 'Romance' dissolves in the face of 'nature'. The parody of *Pamela* in *Joseph Andrews* has developed into the more widespread general parodies of *Tom Jones*, but in both cases they are founded upon a confident sense of the way the world works, and the ways that people (young men especially) behave within it.

If Fielding's novels can be defined by their parodic distance

from other, repudiated kinds of writing, that is equally a definition that can be applied to the novels of Jane Austen; here, too,
parody has a central role in the novels in marking their distance
from the stigmatised forms. Indeed, her biographer John Halperin
describes her as coming to literary flower in the 1790s 'principally
as a parodist' (Halperin, 1986: 66); her Juvenilia, including the
splendid 'Love and Friendship', consist of a series of parodies of a
range of contemporary novelistic styles. Traces of parody remain
throughout her work – in *Pride and Prejudice*, for example, which
may well have been the first of her novels to be written (under the
title 'First Impressions'), and which even in its published form
shows affinities to those youthful parodic exercises. Parody is most
evident in another early novel, *Northanger Abbey* (written in 1803
but published posthumously in 1818). The conformity of this
novel to our putative history of the genre is sufficiently indicated
from this textbook account: 'The origin of the story is the desire to
ridicule tales of romance and terror such as Mrs. Radcliffe's
"Mysteries of Udolpho" and to contrast with these life as it really
is' (Harvey, 1967: 583). Once again we can see how the novelness
of Jane Austen's work is constituted by its distance from
'romance', here more specifically the Gothic romances popular at
the end of the eighteenth century and the beginning of the nineteenth century. As in *Don Quixote*, parody is deployed to indicate a
false or infected mentality; the heroine, Catherine Morland, mis-
recognises the world because her head has been filled with the
falsifying and romanticising ideas of Gothic novels.

If the role of parody is especially evident in *Northanger Abbey*,
it can be understood as policing the fringes of Austen's other novels also, above all in the novelist's famous irony, which raises a
doubt about so much of her prose. Ironic discourse is, to use a
phrase of Bakhtin's, 'double-voiced': it permits the reader to
recognise that there are two distinct consciousnesses operating in
a single utterance, and that their evaluative attitudes are not the
same. Thus *Pride and Prejudice* famously begins: 'It is a truth uni-

versally acknowledged, that a single man in possession of a good
fortune, must be in want of a wife'; we can recognise here that we
are being offered a piece of common wisdom which is simultaneously being subjected to some scepticism. We can equally recognise that there is parody at work here, understanding parody
broadly, for that 'truth universally acknowledged' polemically
alludes to the commonplaces of a somewhat short-sighted public
opinion. The phrase itself is parodically expressed, glancing at the
pomposities of Johnsonian English, a highly prestigious form of
prose when Austen was writing. In fact, the banalities to which
such prose could descend, in the hands of Johnson's successors,
are persistently parodied throughout the novel in the moralising
remarks of Elizabeth's sister Mary. The irony of Jane Austen's
prose, therefore, so important in indicating the distance between
mystified ideas and 'life as it really is', is dependent upon a pervasive if lightly indicated capacity for parody.

The mode is similarly present at the margins of much nineteenth-century realist fiction, indicating other generic paths that
the author might have followed, or which she or he is repudiating. Even the work of the most consistently 'realist' novelist of
the century, George Eliot, is hedged about by potentially parodic
generic disclaimers, especially at the beginning of her career.
Thus in her very first work of fiction, 'The Sad Fortunes of the
Rev. Amos Barton', she anticipates the hostility of a 'lady reader'
to her commonplace tale, 'Mrs Farthingale, for example, who
prefers the ideal in fiction; to whom tragedy means ermine tip-
pets, adultery, and murder; and comedy, the adventures of some
personage who is quite a "character"' (Eliot, 1973: Chapter 5).
Parody is skirting the borders of this fiction, indicating the
author's repudiation of falsifying genres in favour of the aggressively commonplace nature of her own writing.

But the nineteenth-century novelist who is most heavily
dependent upon parody is undoubtedly W.M. Thackeray, who
persistently uses the mode to establish the legitimacy of his own

writing as against the delusive claims of the debased, 'romantic' genres which encroach upon it. It is significant that he is also a novelist who, in his capacity as a comic journalist for *Punch* in the 1840s, provided a series of set-piece specific parodies of contemporary novelists called 'Novels by Eminent Hands'. Thackeray's targets were Bulwer Lytton, Benjamin Disraeli, Charles Lever, G.P.R. James, the anonymous authoress of a 'silver-fork' novel (a genre of gushing fantasy about aristocratic life), and Fenimore Cooper; he even offers a parodic version of himself. But it is more important to recognise that he was attacking, not so much specific novelists, as whole kinds of novel, such as the military or historical romance, or romances of high life, or the Newgate novel (melodramatic crime novels which he saw as romanticising crime); more generally, he attacked novels written in pretentious and idealising style.

Here is an excerpt from 'Barbazure', Thackeray's parody of the historical romances (after Walter Scott) of G.P.R. James:

Like many another fabric of feudal war and splendour, the once vast and magnificent Castle of Barbazure is now a moss-grown ruin ... In the days of our tale its turrets and pinnacles rose as stately, and seemed (to the pride of sinful man!) as strong as the eternal rocks on which they stood. The three mullets on a gule wavy reversed, surmounted by the sinople couchant Or, the well-known cognisance of the house, blazed in gorgeous heraldry on a hundred banners, surmounting as many towers. The long lines of battlemented walls spread down the mountain to the Loire, and were defended by thousands of steel-clad serving-men. Four hundred knights, and six times as many archers fought round the banner of Barbazure at Bouvines, Malplaquet, and Azincour. For his services at Fontenoy against the English, the heroic Charles Martel appointed the fourteenth Baron Hereditary Grand Bootjack of the kingdom of France; and for wealth, and for splendour, and for skill and fame in war, Raoul, the twenty-eighth Baron, was in nowise inferior to his noble ancestors.

That the Baron Raoul levied toll upon the river and mail upon the shore; that he now and then ransomed a burgher, plundered a neighbour, or drew the fangs of a Jew; that he burned an enemy's castle with the wife and children within; – these were points for which the country knew and respected the stout baron.

(Thackeray, 1877a: 277)

We can see here how the ideological point of the parody emerges from the playfulness of this passage, which begins by imitating James's style, continues by poking fun at the parade of technical heraldic terms, but concludes by a more serious attack on the ethics of feudalism, mistakenly romanticised, we are to understand, by writing such as James's. The polemical point of Thackeray's parodies is especially transparent here, as he seeks to propose some standards by which the falsifying genres may be measured. In 'Rebecca and Rowena', his fanciful and partly parodic rewriting of Scott's *Ivanhoe*, he is explicit about the inadequacies of romance, and about the kinds of novel that should supersede them:

Let us have middle-aged novels, then, as well as your extremely juvenile legends: let the young ones be warned that the old folks have a right to be interesting: and that a lady may continue to have a heart, although she is somewhat stouter than she was when a school-girl, and a man his feelings, although he gets his hair from Truefitt's.

(Thackeray, 1877b: 471)

Thackeray's specific parodies, then, contribute to an aesthetic of the novel which repudiates 'romance' as juvenile, as glamorising feudal military practice, and as inadequate to the humdrum realities of the world. The continuity of this aesthetic with that of Cervantes is apparent, even if it appears in a more definitively bourgeois version in the writing of the mid-nineteenth-century novelist. Furthermore, Thackeray's parodies do not only surround his novels as guard dogs, ready to see off the delusive attractions of romance. They enter into the novels themselves, continually offering alternative generic possibilities which the novels can repudiate. This is truest of his most famous novel, *Vanity Fair*, which is stuffed with parodies both specific and general. Consider, for example, the opening of Chapter VI, 'Vauxhall', in which Thackeray withdraws from the narrative momentarily in order to reflect upon his manner of telling it:

> I know that the tune I am piping is a very mild one (although there are some terrific chapters coming presently), and must beg the good-natured reader to remember, that we are only discoursing at present about a stockbroker's family in Russell Square, who are taking walks, or luncheon, or dinner, or talking, and making love as people do in common life, and without a single passionate and wonderful incident to mark the progress of their loves. The argument stands thus – Osborne, in love with Amelia, has asked an old friend to dinner and to Vauxhall – Jos Sedley is in love with Rebecca. Will he marry her? That is the great subject now in hand.
>
> We might have treated this subject in the genteel, or in the romantic, or in the facetious manner. Suppose we had laid the scene in Grosvenor Square, with the very same adventures – would not some people have listened? Suppose we had shown how Lord Joseph Sedley fell in love, and the Marquis of Osborne became attached to Lady Amelia, with the full consent of the duke, her noble father: or instead of the supremely genteel, suppose we had resorted to the entirely low, and described what was going on in Mr. Sedley's kitchen; – how black Sambo was in love with the cook (as indeed he was), and how he fought a battle with the coachman in her behalf; how the knife-boy was caught stealing a cold shoulder of mutton, and Miss Sedley's new *femme de chambre* refused to go to bed without a wax candle; such incidents might be made to provoke much delightful laughter, and be supposed to represent scenes of 'life'. Or if, on the contrary, we had taken a fancy for the terrible, and made the lover of

the new *femme de chambre* a professional burglar, who burst into the house with his band, slaughters Black Sambo at the feet of his master, and carries off Amelia in his night-dress, not to be let loose again till the third volume, we should easily have constructed a tale of thrilling interest, through the fiery chapters of which the readers should hurry, panting. But my readers must hope for no such romance, only a homely story, and must be content with a chapter about Vauxhall, which is so short that it scarce deserves to be called a chapter at all.

(Thackeray, 1983, 60–1)

In this version of the novel, published in 1853, the parodies here are only lightly suggested, but in the first version, published in part-issue in 1847–8, they were much more extensive, including fully worked-out versions of the parodies of James, Bulwer-Lytton and Eugène Sue indicated here. But even in this truncated form, it is possible to see very clearly the contrast between the repudiated modes of 'romance' and the 'homely story' which Thackeray is offering in their place. The inextricability of these generic questions from questions of class is also apparent in this passage, since the parodied genres – silver-fork novel, comic low-life, and Newgate novel – are all genres which take the extremes of society as their topic, and indeed derive their generic interest from this. By contrast, Thackeray is here insisting on the ordinariness of the lives whose story he is recounting, where ordinary means effectively 'middle-class' as much as commonplace. The novel is the genre, in this powerful manifesto for it, best suited for people 'who are taking walks, or luncheon, or dinner, or talking, and making love as people do in common life'. Parody polices the boundaries of the genre; more strongly, it establishes by contrast the very naturalness to which the novel aspires. If we take seriously the subtitle of *Vanity Fair* – 'A Novel without a Hero' – the purpose of parody in discrediting those genres which aspire to the 'heroic' can be seen as part of the wider generic history of the novel, the form which, above all others, is addressed to 'common life' in all its unheroic ordinariness.

The place of parody in Thackeray's writing by no means ends here. His novels are thick with it, as the thousand forms of discourse which circulate in the mid-nineteenth century are recycled parodically in his fictions, which echo with the burlesqued styles of court-journalism, sentimental poetry, popular piety, affectionate lady-like correspondence, art criticism, schoolbook exercises, religious tracts, and many other fleetingly captured popular expressions, turns of phrase, and tones of voice. However, the central point remains, that this discursive variety serves to reinforce the reliance of the novel, as a form, upon the power of parody to establish its particular claims to truthfulness among the babble of competing voices.

I have taken Fielding, Jane Austen and Thackeray as exemplary of the development of the novel in English, in which parody plays an important role in distinguishing the particular quality of novelistic truthfulness from the claims of the repudiated genres which surround it. Parody is equally important in other national traditions; as just one example, it plays a crucial role in Gustave Flaubert's *Madame Bovary* (1856), where it establishes the inadequacy of the mentality of the inhabitants of provincial France at whom the novel's ferocious ironies are directed. In a famous scene, Flaubert juxtaposes two equally discredited modes of discourse, as the speeches at a provincial agricultural prize-giving are cross-cut with the seduction speeches of Madame Bovary's first lover, Rodolphe:

> 'And that's what you've realised', said the councillor. 'You, farmers and workers in the fields! You, pacific pioneers of civilisation's very work! You, men of progress and of morality! You have realised, I say, that political storms are even more dangerous really than the disorders of the atmosphere ...'
>
> 'Happiness is met one day,' Rodolphe repeated, 'one day, all of a

sudden, when you despaired of it. Then your horizons expand, it's like
a voice which cries "There it is!". You feel the need to entrust to this
person the confidence of your life, to give everything to them, to sacri-
fice everything to them! You don't have to explain yourself, you just
know. You have met before in your dreams.'

(Flaubert, 1972: 196)

Both modes of discourse are subject to parody here, both the public and pompous declamations of the councillor, and the private,
hackneyed and wholly calculated expressions of the lover. The
juxtaposition of the two parodies works to ferocious effect, emp-
tying out both discourses of any sense of truth or affective
import. But parody in *Madame Bovary* is more fundamental even
than this set-piece scene suggests, for this is the novel above all
which sets out to expose the mentality of its principal characters,
whose minds are seen to be filled, without exception, with the
stupidities and false expectations of a provincial bourgeois civilisation. Parody is the means of indicating this mentality, as the
thoughts and speeches of these characters relentlessly expose
themselves as full of clichés, pomposities and second-hand
phrases. A pervasive irony permits this to be visible, as in the
scene I have quoted, without the explicit intervention of Flaubert
to indicate this to the reader.

These are just some indications of the place of parody in the
history of the nineteenth-century novel. We can carry forward our
putative history of the novel into the twentieth century, where
the novel has continued to feed off stigmatised genres as a way of
establishing its own particular truthfulness – though we would
have to extend our list of such genres to include not just the persistent possibilities of 'romance', but also the debased vocabularies of popular journalism, advertising, and the mass media more
generally. This is especially evident in the tradition of comic
writing in English which includes Evelyn Waugh and Muriel
Spark, but the use of parody to police the boundaries of novelistic

seriousness is apparent also in the work of the eminently non-comic writer, Doris Lessing. Thus Evelyn Waugh's novels, *Vile Bodies* (1930) and *Scoop* (1938), are marked at intervals by parodies of the lying languages of journalism, memoirs, gossip columns, and both Bolshevik and Fascist rhetoric. A particular pleasure in the latter novel is the frequent parody of journalists' telegrams: 'OPPOSITION SPLASHING FRONTWARD SPEEDILIEST STOP ADEN REPORTED PREPARED WARWISE FLASH FACTS BEAST' (Waugh 1943: 68), but the pervasive irony of the novel serves to undercut the language of journalism more widely than this, as is only appropriate in a novel which satirises the journalistic profession. Equally, Muriel Spark's *The Girls of Slender Means* (1963), set in part in the literary world of London at the end of the Second World War, relies at intervals upon parodies of the habitual attitudes and language of this world, and also upon a more widespread irony at the expense of the characteristic valuations of this milieu, as in the first sentence of the novel: 'Long ago in 1945 all the nice people in England were poor, allowing for exceptions.' We can read this in the same way that we read the opening sentence of *Pride and Prejudice*, as a parody of a widespread opinion which is not the author's, and indeed at the end of the paragraph the same phrase is repeated, but glossed as a 'general axiom' held up for ironic inspection (Spark, 1963: 1). In a more extended way, we may note the use of parody by Doris Lessing in *The Golden Notebook* (1963), which can be seen as a massive experiment in different possible ways of writing a novel, and which includes parodic versions of film treatments of a novel written by the novelist's heroine, with parody again serving as an indication of a stigmatised genre from which the novel itself takes its distance.

Finally, to indicate the continuing pervasiveness of parody in the novel, there is the following excerpt from Jonathan Coe's *What a Carve Up!* (1994), a comic *tour d'horizon* of post-war England, centred upon the monstrous Winshaw family. One of them is

Hilary Winshaw, a Thatcherite popular journalist of ruthless ambition; having had a baby, she is interviewed for *Hello!* magazine:

HILARY WINSHAW AND SIR PETER EAVES

Husband-and-wife team are so happy with baby Josephine but
'our love for each other didn't need strengthening'

Maternal love shines out of Hilary Winshaw's eyes as she lifts her giggling one-month-old daughter Josephine high in the air in the conservatory of the happy couple's lovely South Kensington home. They've waited a long time for their first child – Hilary and Sir Peter were married almost six years ago, when they met on the newspaper which he continues to edit and for which she still writes a popular weekly column – but, as Hilary told *Hello!* in this exclusive interview, Josephine was well worth waiting for!

Tell us, Hilary, how did you feel when you first saw your baby daughter?

Well, exhausted, for one thing! I suppose by most people's standards it was an easy labour but I certainly don't intend to go through it again in a hurry! But one glimpse of Josephine and it all seemed worthwhile. It was an amazing feeling.

(Coe, 1995: 78–9)

In case the reader should be in any doubt about the true state of Hilary's feeling towards the baby, the parody of *Hello!* is followed by this exchange between the mother and the child's nanny:

Hilary stared malevolently at her daughter, watching her face crumple as she gathered breath for another scream.
    '*Now* what's the matter with it?' she said.
    'Just wind, I think,' said the nanny.

Hilary fanned herself with the menu.

'Well can't you take it outside for a while? It's showing us up in front of everybody.'

(ibid.: 80)

The juxtaposition of the two passages is sufficient to discredit the parodied writing of *Hello!*; not unlike Thackeray's novels, in fact, *What a Carve Up!* is full of the diverse languages of the contemporary world, many of them drawn from popular or commercial culture. This too is a novel which can confidently switch from a parodied and inauthentic language to one which reveals more accurately the contours of the world we actually inhabit.

Taking these writers, from Cervantes to Thackeray and Flaubert, and from Austen to Waugh, Spark, Lessing and Coe, as exemplary, we have succeeded in constructing a history of the novel in which parody is central. This history is cognate with one powerful tradition of novel-criticism – in which the novel is defined by its distance from 'romance' or other stigmatised genres, and which operates with a confident and normative notion of realism. Parody serves the purposes of realism in this account, because it holds up to ridicule those falsifying genres which offer wonder and wish-fulfilment in the place of sober realism. To measure the absurdities of the repudiated genres, the novel instead offers a model of sober and natural prose which is better fitted to the realities of 'life as it is'. Furthermore, parody is used as a powerful device in the culture wars which surround writing; conflicts over genre are inextricably linked with conflicts over class, as we saw especially in the cases of Cervantes, Fielding and Thackeray. Parody in the novel – a one-sided conclusion, but a true one – is a weapon wielded on behalf of sturdy common sense, and against the attractions of self-delusion and make-believe, however exalted their origin.

THE HISTORY OF THE NOVEL IN ANOTHER ASPECT

There are, however, several aspects of this 'history of the novel', and the place of parody in it, which might give one pause. There is, for example, a certain arbitrariness in beginning a history of the modern European novel with Cervantes, rather than with Rabelais, who was writing some sixty or seventy years before the publication of *Don Quixote*. Rabelais's influence on the subsequent history of the novel is at least as great as Cervantes's, and his use of parody, though very different, is just as central to his writing. Moreover, the account I have given fails to investigate the generic roots of *Don Quixote* itself; perhaps its parodic practice develops out of some other and profoundly popular 'pre-novelistic' cultural practices. Third, even within the novels that I have included in my putative history, the practice of parody is not as relentlessly negative and normative as I have made it appear. The English critic George Saintsbury once described Thackeray as providing both 'romance, and satire of romance'; perhaps some such ambivalence is more widespread in, and characteristic of, the novel tradition than I have allowed.

But the most telling reason for recognising the one-sidedness of that constitutively 'anti-romantic' history of the novel is the fact that it requires a very particular *selection* from the novelistic tradition to sustain it. It may not have escaped your attention that some of the repudiated genres which 'novels' parody and repudiate are themselves novelistic ones: the novels of Richardson, Gothic, Newgate, 'silver-fork', military-historical, and sensation novels. In short, my one-sided history of the novel, based as it is on a strong tradition of novel criticism in English, is a fiercely normative and selective one. I might even go so far as to say that the previous section of this chapter was a *parody*.

It is certainly possible to tell a different story with respect to the novel and parody, even using the same body of evidence. This other story is a more Bakhtinian one, in which the novel's relationship to other genres is not solely hostile – for the novel has a capacity to devour other genres with varying degrees of parody. Bakhtin indeed speaks of a 'competition between the genres', but the work of the novel, in this more inclusive view, is not so much normative as sceptical and relativising. Perhaps it is not the false-ness of parodied genres that makes them subject to attack, but their one-sided seriousness; the true enemy of the chivalric romance in *Don Quixote* is not 'realism' but Sancho Panza's appetite-driven humanity. Novelistic parody, in this second more inclusive account, does not simply cancel those genres which it attacks; it includes them among the possible voices in a competi-tive babble out of which the novel is constituted.

This more all-embracing view also leads us to reconsider those cultural conflicts in which novelistic parody takes on its specific force. One of the difficulties of that one-sided 'history of the novel' was that it could be resolved into a history of the conflict between truth and error; in other words it is a deeply ideological account in which a principle of sober realism embodied in the novel is constantly battling against the forces of delusion and wish-fulfilment embodied in romance in its various generic man-ifestations. If on the contrary we see the novel as mobilising the full range of discursive possibilities of any given period, and drawing upon specific popular energies to do so, we have perhaps the ground for a more fully historical account of parody, and not only as it operates in the novel.

Thus as far as *Don Quixote* is concerned, we need not only rely on that moment in the Prologue when Cervantes invokes a sim-ple notion of 'imitation' to help us understand the resources upon which the novel is drawing. Parody of the chivalric romance was not, in fact, invented by Cervantes; there is a popular ballad farce, pre-dating the novel, which equally features a man obsessed by such romances, and which is indeed cited as one of its 'sources'. And if Sancho Panza is the true antidote to the chivalric romance, then it would seem that Cervantes is invoking the practice of popular laughter in his parodies as much as more scholarly and normative canons of realism. Finally, we can glance back to long traditions of serio-comic writing, stretching back through the medieval period to the ancient world, in which parody has played a central place. In this greatly expanded context for the novel, it can be seen as a site in which multiple discourses are put into play; novels take their energy from the particular eruption of popular laughter that characterises Early Modern Europe. Parody, in this account, is much less simply negative and conservative, much more fully generous and relativising.

Comparable corrections need to be made for many of the examples that I adduced, bringing to bear, not so much the force of truth against error, as the particular play of discursive forces which surround the novels I have discussed. Thus in reconsidering the case of Thackeray, we would have to consider the particular milieu out of which his writing emerged in the late 1830s and 1840s: the world of comic magazines and mildly Bohemian journalism of which *Punch* is the best known product. This is a world in which discourses circulate and are recycled at high speed, in which a multitude of forms jostle and compete with each other, and in which everything is subject to parody in varying degrees of hostility. Thus while it is certainly true to say that Thackeray habitually contrasts 'romance' to some more recalcitrant principle at work in the world and represented in novels (and he is especially likely to do so at moments of reflective seriousness), it is also true that there is a more playful impulse at work in his writing which takes great pleasure in the myriad discourses included. His parodies, in fact, do not always suggest 'realism' as the normative other, but rather a pleasure in the variety of discourse coupled, at times, with a more subversive scepticism about all discursive forms. In this his novels can be thought of as reproducing, in their own distinctive ways, the discursive competition which characterised the magazines from which they emerged.

So while it is certainly possible to tell the history of the novel in the way that I have done, it is also a very partial way of doing so, and a fuller account of the place of parody in this story would recognise a much more inclusive ambivalence as characteristic of it. Moreover, to insist on a principle of 'realism' as the normative other typically suggested by parody is to recruit the mode too simply to that conservative 'policing' function which is certainly one of its aspects but not the only one. We can get a very different story, much more open to the comic and destabilising capacities of parody, if we tell the story of the European novel not as passing from Cervantes through Fielding, Austen and Thackeray into the twentieth century, but as passing from Rabelais, Sterne's *Tristram Shandy* and on to Joyce's *Ulysses*.

Let us consider the place of parody in the novel from this other perspective, in which the function of the mode is not normative but destabilising, for if one discursive form can be parodied, perhaps all discourse can be, and there is no secure ground of knowledge on which we can rest. The alternative novelistic tradition which runs from Rabelais to Joyce, and forward into the present in the work of Salman Rushdie and Patrick Chamoiseau, is learned, scatological, fantastic, and wildly inclusive of discursive styles drawn from all directions, high and low, academic and popular. It makes extensive use of parody in multiple ways as it assimilates, assaults and lovingly reproduces the diverse verbal materials out of which it is constituted. It is also interesting that this tradition has had a kind of shadow existence alongside the tradition of the novel as I first sketched it. This is in part because its vulgarity and bodily realism have meant that many of the novels of this tradition have had a chequered publishing history, including suppression, private publication, and prosecution for obscenity. But it is also because they may be thought of as 'anti-novels', in which the very sustaining conventions of narrative, and thus of the novel itself, are parodied: such matters as narrative continuity and chronological progression, consistency of 'character', and confidence in the ability of language to refer successfully to the world as it is.

Rabelais's great novel from the mid-sixteenth century (the four books of which are entitled *Gargantua*, *Pantagruel*, and then the Third and Fourth Books), provides the best starting-point for considering this tradition, but these writings themselves spring from popular-cultural and learned practices that long pre-date the books' actual publication. Rabelais's writings are at once learned and a satire upon learning; they swing wildly from parodic scholarly lists compiled at ludicrous length, to celebrations of the gargantuan guzzlings, belchings, pissings and evacuations of the giant bodies who inhabit the novel. Bakhtin suggests that the social and historical ground for this writing is the late medieval and Early Modern ensemble of cultural practices known as carnival, characterised by feasting, popular festivities, and the mockery of all that is official and sacred. If he is correct, Rabelais's writing reproduces, in its parodies, some of those popular-festive attitudes which hold the discourse of the official world up to ridicule. We can consider the following parody of learned discourse in this context; it comes in Chapter 6 of *Pantagruel* – 'How Pantagruel met with a Limosin, who affected to speak in learned phrase':

> 'My friend,' [asked Pantagruel,] 'from whence comest thou now?' The scholar answered him, 'From the *alme*, *inclyte*, and celebrate academy, which is *vocitated Lutetia*.' 'What is the meaning of this?' said Pantagruel to one of his men. 'It is', answered he, 'from Paris.' 'Thou comest from Paris, then,' said Pantagruel; 'and how do you spend your time there, you, my masters, the students of Paris?' The *scholar* answered, 'We *transfretate* the *sequan* at the *dilucal* and *crepuscul*; we *deambulate* by the *compites* and *quadrines* of the *urb*; we *despumate* the *latial verbocination*; and like *verisimilarie amorabons*, we *captat* the benevolence of the *omnijugal*, *omniform*, and *omnigenal fœminine sex*; upon certain *diecules* we *invisat* the *lupanares*, and in a *venerian extase inculcate* our *veretres*, into the *penetissime recesses* of the *pudends* of these *amicabilissim meretricules*.
>
> (Rabelais, n.d.: 134)

This is slightly complicated by the nineteenth-century translation, which renders Pantagruel's own speech into now antiquated
forms ('Thou comest …', etc.). Nevertheless, the point of the parody is plain enough. It is an assault on the barbarous Latinate jargon of scholars, who insist upon rendering French words into
quasi-Latin equivalents. Close readers with some knowledge at
least of cod Latin might also have recognised the ribald meaning
of the scholar's last sentence. This is a typical learned joke at the
expense of learning, not unlike the various macaronic and pig
Latins once relished by schoolchildren. But the grounds of
Rabelais's assault are very different, as Pantagruel's reaction to the
scholar's jargon makes clear:

> 'By G—,' said Pantagruel, 'I will teach you to speak: but first come
> hither, and tell me whence thou art?' To this the scholar answered:
> 'The *primeval origin* of my *aves* and *ataves* was *indigenary* of the
> *Lemovick* regions, where *requiesceth* the *corpor* of the *hagiotat* St.
> Martial.' 'I understand thee very well,' said Pantagruel; 'when all
> comes to all, thou art a Limosin, and thou wilt here, by thy affected
> speech, counterfeit the Parisians. Well now, come hither; I must show
> thee a new trick, and handsomely give thee one fling.' With this he
> took him by the throat, saying to him, 'Thou flayest the Latin; by St.
> John, I will make thee flay the fox, for I will now flay thee alive.' Then
> began the poor Limosin to cry: 'Haw, gwid maaster! haw, Laord, my
> halp and St. Marshaw! haw, I am worried: my thropple, the bean of
> my cragg is bruk: haw, for Guaad's seck, lawt me lean, mawster; waw,
> waw, waw.' 'Now,' said Pantagruel, 'thou speakest naturally;' and so
> let him go: for the poor Limosin had totally bewrayed and thoroughly
> conshit his breeches, which were not deep and large, but made *à
> queüe de merlus*.
>
> (Rabelais, n.d.: 135)

Under threat of violence from Pantagruel, the scholar reverts
from his affected jargon into a more 'natural' dialect, that of his

native Limosin, suggested here by the cod Barsetshire of ' "Haw, gwid maaster ..." '. The parody of scholarly affectation, then, emerges from the babble of conflicting dialects in sixteenth-century France, a linguistic world in a period of fluid transition and where there is no accepted standard dialect. It is cut across equally by the conflict between the dialects of Paris and of Limoges. Pantagruel's impatience is enforced so thoroughly that the poor scholar shits himself – a reminder, in Bakhtin's words, of the lower bodily stratum, the gay matter from which we come and to which we will return – the necessary counterpart to the high-faluting language of the scholar. In short, in these extracts from Rabelais, parody is indeed being deployed in a polemical spirit, against a particular version of French based upon a pretentious copying of Latin; but the more 'natural' version of the language offered in place of this stigmatised form is not some normative correctness, but one of a number of possible popular dialects in competition with each other. In this context, the parodied language takes its place among a babble of languages, nicely reproduced in the translation above. The novel thus becomes the form which is most open to this linguistic diversity, and parody is but one of the ways in which particular discourses make their entry into it.

Rabelais's writing is derived from several sources, some, as we have seen, popular-cultural, others from various learned kinds of writing, like the menippea of antiquity, and the *parodia sacra* of the medieval world (there is considerable controversy about whether these themselves have roots in the popular-festive world of the carnival). Carrying forward our alternative history of the novel, we can jump directly to Laurence Sterne, whose *Life and Opinions of Tristram Shandy* (1759–67) similarly draws upon various serio-comic modes, and in which parody also plays a central role. In Chapter XIX of Volume VI of *Tristram Shandy*, Tristram's father, Mr Shandy senior, consults one of his books to help him decide in what fashion of breeches to dress his son. Since children are breeched at about the age of 4, and the novel has already reached near the end of the seventh volume (out of nine), it can be seen that the novel's length has far outpaced the span of the life from which it takes its title. However, Shandy's textbook does not help him much, for it is a volume concerned with the dress of the ancient Romans:

> Upon every other article of ancient dress, *Rubenius* was very communicative to my father;- gave him a full and satisfactory account of
>
>   The Toga, or loose gown.
>   The Chlamys.
>   The Ephod.
>   The Tunica, or Jacket.
>   The Synthesis.
>   The Pænula.
>   The Lacerna, with its Cucullus.
>   The Paludamentum.
>   The Prætexta.
>   The Sagum, or soldier's jerkin.
>   The Trabea: of which, according to Suetonius, there were
>   three kinds. –
>
> – But what are all these to the breeches? said my father.
>
> (Sterne, 1997: 364–5)

A fair question, for *Rubenius* continues with a similar list for different kinds of Roman shoe, with information on the materials and colours of the clothes, on the fulling and dyeing processes that affected Roman garments, with an account of Roman holiday wear, and with a learned dispute on the meaning of the *Latus Clavus* or stripe on the senatorial toga (Sterne lists the disputants). This chapter is a typical one, for the novel as a whole is replete with this learned parody of learning, Sterne delighting in the display of useless knowledge, and the text progressing by such digressions. Indeed, it is foolish to describe them as digressions, for they make up the substance of the book, which is in one sense an ensemble of parodic writings.

However, even this account of the novel will not do, because it makes it sound too much like a collection of unconnected fragments. On the contrary, while it certainly displays no 'deep-breathing unity and organic form' in the manner that Henry James recommends, *Tristram Shandy* is in part a parody of the very principles by which narratives are constructed. Thus in the final chapter of the same volume in which the parody of Shandy senior's Roman learning appears, Sterne promises to continue his narrative in a more straightforward way, which he represents as a straight line drawn across the page:

He concedes that previous volumes have been more circuitous, which he represents by a series of squiggly lines. Sterne confronts here, as he does in numerous other places throughout the novel, the impossibility of 'straightforward' narrative. That is to say, he invites his readers to consider the incompatibility between the multiplicity of human experience and the linearity of narrative. If he does so in this instance in comic and diagrammatic form, he does so elsewhere in the novel by its most fundamental parody, namely of the possibility of recounting a human life at all.

Tristram has not yet been breeched and the novel is nearly two-thirds complete. This is in keeping with a book in which the hero takes a volume to get conceived, and another three to be born – 'From this moment', he writes at the end of Volume IV, 'I am to be considered as heir-apparent to the *Shandy* family – and it is from this point properly, that the story of my LIFE and OPINIONS sets out' (Sterne, 1997: 277). In fact, in order appropriately to explain the circumstances attending such actions as conception and birth, Sterne (or rather Shandy himself, for this is a first-person narrative), has to go back and explain so many other circumstances that there is a real possibility that the story will never be told, and that the time taken to tell it will outrun the time available, as the narrator will never be able to catch up with himself. The parody here, then, is comically metafictive (drawing attention to its own fictiveness), ceaselessly confronting the conditions of its own possibility, and with that the possibility of narrative itself.

If this is the most fundamental consideration to which the parodies in *Tristram Shandy* propel us, in other ways also the novel continues the tradition of Rabelais. It too is full of incidental parodies, as of the conventions of Preface and Dedication, which allow Sterne to insert an all-purpose Dedication at the end of Chapter VIII of the First Volume:

My Lord,

'I maintain this to be a dedication, notwithstanding its singularity in the three great essentials of matter, form and place: I beg, therefore, you will accept it as such, and that you will permit me to lay it, with the most respectful humility, at your Lordship's feet, – when you are upon them – which you can be when you please – and that is, my Lord, when ever there is occasion for it, and I will add, to the best purposes too. I have the honour to be,

> *My Lord,*
> *Your Lordship's most obedient,*
> *and most devoted,*
> *and most humble servant,*
> TRISTRAM SHANDY'

The parody of the fawning style of dedication is plain enough here; especially enjoyable is the way that the dedicator gets into a tangle with the metaphor of his Lordship's feet, and proceeds to seek to correct himself, but only manages to make matters worse and worse until he extricates himself with the magnificently empty '... to the best purposes too'. The whole novel is full of such parodies, as it is of the special jargons of law, scholarship, warfare, obstetrics, and religion. As we have seen, the ground for these multiple parodic celebrations of the varieties of language is not some confidence that, out of its fantastic garb, discourse can represent nature; on the contrary, the novel proliferates from a comic scepticism concerning the very bases upon which all stories, and therefore all novels, are constructed.

One can trace a continuation of this novelistic tradition in English in the nineteenth century, though it appears in more scholarly and less ribald forms, as in the novels and symposia of Thomas Love Peacock, Carlyle and W.H. Mallock. In all of these, parody plays a crucial role in representing, in serio-comic form, some of the central intellectual preoccupations of the period. But this whole alternative tradition of the novel erupts most powerfully in English in the writing of Joyce, whose *Ulysses* (1922) can be seen as a compendium of the discursive possibilities of early twentieth-century Ireland (and perhaps Britain also), in which parody plays a central role.

Initially, we can see a kind of parody at work in the way that Joyce represents the so-called 'stream of consciousness' of Leopold Bloom. Unlike the very different techniques of other Modernist writers such as Virginia Woolf or May Sinclair, Joyce assembles the consciousness of Bloom out of scraps of discourse, random phrases and tags of contemporary idiom, which are held together partly by an associative 'psychological' logic, but are also partly arbitrary. Thus as Bloom makes his way around Dublin, his mind is filled with the phrases, slogans, and sounds that he meets, as in the following example when he is travelling in the funeral cortège of Paddy Dignam:

> As they turned into Berkely street a streetorgan near the basin sent over and after them a rollicking rattling song of the halls. Has anybody here seen Kelly? Kay ee double ell wy. Dead march from *Saul*.

> He's as bad as old Antonio. He left me on my ownio. Pirouette! The *Mater Misericordiae*. Eccles street. My house down there. Big place. Ward for incurables there. Very encouraging. Our Lady's Hospice for the dying. Deadhouse handy underneath. Where old Mrs Riordan died. They look terrible the women. Her feeding cup and rubbing her mouth with the spoon. Then the screen round her bed for her to die. Nice young student that was dressed that bite the bee gave me. He's gone over to the lying-in hospital they told me. From one extreme to the other.

(Joyce, 1968: 99)

This is scarcely parody, though there is the ironic repetition, within Bloom's consciousness, of popular-cultural phrases randomly encountered ('Has anybody here seen Kelly? Kay ee double ell wy.'), and of the clichés of everyday discourse which he arrives at on his own account ('From one extreme to the other.'). Vološinov's account of the operation of consciousness, and its constitution out of the words of another, constantly recycled in the to-and-fro of discourse, seems to me to be very helpful as an analogue for the way Joyce imagines the operation of Bloom's consciousness here (Vološinov, 1976). They are both accounts which teeter on the verge of parody as the extent and depth of penetration of socially established discursive fragments, into the mentality of the character, are suggested.

More fully parodic is Joyce's inclusion, in many diverse ways, of more extended scraps of the many discourses circulating in Dublin at the beginning of the century – of nationalism, religion, homely piety, British imperialism, the slangs of journalism, literary criticism and so forth. Thus in the episode which immediately follows the funeral, Bloom visits the newspaper office of the *Dublin Telegraph* and listens in on the conversation of a gathering of journalists and other writers. Their talk is arbitrarily broken up by sub-headings ('IN THE HEART OF THE HIBERNIAN METROPOLIS', for example), which themselves are parodies of a certain style of journalese. But their talk is also made up of the clichés, set phrases and familiar jokes which are part of the ready cynicism of their trade. At times the text rises to formal parody, as when one of the participants in the conversation, Professor MacHugh, recalls a moment of fine nationalist oratory from a university debating society; its premise is the analogy between the Irish under British rule, and the Jews in Egyptian captivity, and I take it up at its climax:

A dumb belch of hunger cleft his speech. He lifted his voice above it boldly:

– But, ladies and gentlemen, had the youthful Moses listened to and accepted that view of life, had he bowed his head and bowed his will and bowed his spirit before that arrogant admonition he would never have brought the chosen people out of their house of bondage nor followed the pillar of the cloud by day. He would never have spoken with the Eternal amid lightnings on Sinai's mountaintop nor ever have come down with the light of inspiration shining in his countenance and bearing in his arms the tables of the law, graven in the language of the outlaw.

He ceased and looked at them, enjoying silence.

OMINOUS – FOR HIM!

J.J. O'Molloy said not without regret:

– And yet he died without having entered the land of promise.

– A sudden-at-the-moment-though-from-lingering-illness-often-previously-expectorated-demise, Lenehan said. And with a great future behind him.

(Joyce, 1968: 143–4)

The force of the parody of the nationalist oration is at least ambivalent here; it certainly is a good enough speech to win the respectful silence of its immediate audience, and cannot simply be described as an assault on the kind of high-flown rhetoric which it uses. And yet it is surrounded by various deflating indications, not least the 'belch of hunger' which punctuates it, and Lenehan's jokey reference to the orator's death – which itself is a parodic transformation of the language of 'Death Notices' to be found in newspapers. The parodies here, then, indicate the jostling competition of discourses out of which the novel is constituted, and do not suggest any single authoritative or master discourse which might measure their inadequacies.

The most fully developed parodies in the novel, however, occur in the 'Oxen of the Sun' episode, when Bloom visits the lying-in hospital to enquire about the well-being of Mrs Purefoy. While there he falls in with Stephen Dedalus and a drunken party of medical students; the whole episode is conducted through a series of parodies which amount to a résumé of the history of English prose, starting with a parodic translation of medieval Latin, and passing through Early Modern English, various parodies of seventeenth-, eighteenth- and nineteenth-century prose, and culminating in an extraordinary section, where the prose almost collapses into a miscellaneous mixture of tags and fragments drawn from innumerable varieties of contemporary English, dialect, mimicked accents, and cod Latin. In the course of this journey, more specific parodies emerge, of Bunyan, Swift, Sterne, Burke, Dickens, Ruskin, Carlyle, and so on, though these are not generally hostile. Since the whole topic of the episode is provoked by the matter of Mrs Purefoy's lying-in, the various parodies concern the various phases of human generation, from sexual intercourse to parturition, a developmental sequence which is perhaps paralleled by the story told, via parody, of the development (and degeneration) of English prose. Here is a characteristically obscene example, the parody of *The Pilgrim's Progress*:

> This was it what all that company that sat there at commons in manse of Mothers the most lusted after and if they met with this whore Bird-in-the-Hand (which was within all foul plagues, monsters

and a wicked devil) they would strain the last but they wold make at her and know her. For regarding Believe-on-Me they said it was nought else but notion and they could conceive no thought of it for, first, Two-in-the-Bush whither she ticed them was the very goodliest grot and in it were four pillows on which were four tickets with these words printed on them, Pickaback and Topsyturvy and Shameface and Cheek by Jowl and, second, for that foul plague Allpox and the monsters they cared not for them, for Preservative had given them a stout shield of oxengut and, third, that they might take no hurt neither from Offspring that was that wicked devil by virtue of that same shield which was named Killchild.

(Joyce, 1968: 393)

The whole episode, which is a matter of some forty or more pages, is conducted via parodies in a similar vein.

One of the first commentators on *Ulysses*, Stuart Gilbert, has commented of these parodies that 'the greater part seem to be devoid of satiric intention; that wilful exaggeration of mannerisms which points a parody is absent and the effect is rather of pastiche than of travesty' (Gilbert, 1969: 255). These distinctions, as we have seen, are hard to sustain in any hard and fast way, though the main point is clear enough: that the parodies are not conducted in a satiric register. However, the overall effect, especially given the climactic descent, in this episode, into a discursive confusion, is one of the instability of the various styles through which the episode passes, an effect quite in keeping with the menippean character of the whole novel.

We can recognise a further level of parody in *Ulysses*, to which the newspaper style sub-headings in this section of the novel point us. This concerns the whole organisation of the novel, which is written in a multiplicity of modes which perhaps begin as parody, but move us into a different terrain in which we are confronted with the fundamental arbitrariness of all modes of discourse. Thus the nighttown section of the novel is written in the form of a playscript, with dialogue and stage-directions taken to a parodic excess of Bosch-like horror:

> *(The famished snaggletusks of an elderly bawd protrude from a door-way.)*
>
> THE BAWD: *(Her voice whispering huskily)* Sst! Come here till I tell you. Maidenhead inside. Sst.
>
> (Joyce, 1968: 427)

And the final meeting between Bloom and Stephen is narrated via a series of ludicrously grandiloquent questions and answers, parodying the false precision of a certain style of academic English:

> Of what did the duumvirate deliberate during their itinerary?
>
> Music, literature, Ireland, Dublin, Paris, friendship, woman, prostitution, diet, the influence of gaslight or the light of the arc and glowlamps on the growth of adjoining paraheliotropic trees, exposed corporation emergency dustbuckets, the Roman catholic church, ecclesiastical celibacy, the Irish nation, jesuit education, careers, the study of medicine, the past day, the maleficent influence of the presabbath, Stephen's collapse.
>
> Did Bloom discover common factors of similarity between their respective like and unlike reactions to experience?
>
> Both were sensitive to artistic impressions musical in preference to plastic or pictorial...
>
> (Joyce, 1968: 586)

In some respects this repeats the learned satire upon learning that we have seen to characterise this tradition since before Rabelais – in this instance by the use of a comically expanded list, and by the employment of a polysyllabic English ('adjoining paraheliotropic trees', etc.) which can be bathetically deflated. The overall effect of these striking shifts of discursive mode, however, is to suggest the relativity of all discourse, in a manner as fundamental as that of Rabelais and Sterne. Parody here has become radically destabilising, suggesting that all discourses are contingently (that is to say socially) constructed.

Finally, reference should be made to the overarching intertextual allusion that the novel makes, via its title, to Homer's *Odyssey*, the topic of elaborate exposition by scholars since the novel's publication. The episode from which I have just quoted, Bloom's meeting with Stephen in the penultimate section of the novel, is the equivalent in Homer's narrative to Ulysses's reunion with Telemachus near the end of the *Odyssey*. Does the novel as a whole have a parodic relation to Homer's hypotext? This question can be answered in at least two ways. On the one hand, Joyce's work can be read as a modern rewriting of the Greek epic, as an inclusive celebration of a modern everyman whose odyssey encompasses the multifarious details of contemporary urban life. Alternatively, some bathos can indeed be read into the comparison, a sense of the littleness of this life introduced by the allusion. It is worth recalling that this ambivalence reproduces the ambivalent polemical direction that we saw in Chapter 1 as characterising parody as a mode.

The alternative tradition represented by Rabelais, Sterne, and Joyce, has continued into the late twentieth century in the writings of such novelists as Salman Rushdie and Patrick Chamoiseau, both, significantly, writers from postcolonial countries. I shall be discussing Rushdie's work more fully in Chapter 6. For now we need to reflect upon some of the consequences of this rewriting of the history of the novel, and the place of parody within it. If in the previous section, in the 'one-sided history of the novel', parody's function had above all been normative, in this other more inclusive version, parody points, not to the possibility of a better way of saying things, but to the possibility that all ways of saying things are equally arbitrary. To help us think through parody of this sort, we need to draw on thinkers whose scepticism does not stop short at the inadequacies of one discourse, but is extended, perhaps, to all of its forms. Bakhtin would certainly be one such thinker, but perhaps Phiddian (see p.15) is right, and we need to draw upon Derrida and Barthes as well.

In this alternative tradition, the role of parody can be interpreted in two alternating ways. On the one hand, hovering at the edges of the mode is to be found, not better sense, but nonsense. Certainly in a wholly other field (though on reflection perhaps not so far from Rabelais), parody was central to the evolution of nonsense poetry in seventeenth-century English verse (see Chapter 4). Reading the writers in this tradition, there is always the possibility that their parodies will tail off into the gobbledegook that perhaps lurks at the margins of all discourse. On the other hand, parody can be a mode of celebration of discursive variety, as the parodied discursive forms take their part in the babble of voices that contend with each other at all moments in history, though perhaps more fully and more benignly at some moments than others. Viewed either way, however, parody in this tradition of the novel is, paradoxically, productive rather than regulative – a paradox only because the greater scepticism about discourse that characterises this tradition produces the more fully and pervasively parodic writing.

But perhaps we ought to abandon the fiction that there are two alternative 'traditions' of the novel which use parody in antithetical ways. At the beginning of this section I suggested that perhaps even the novels I had quoted in my previous one-sided history were more ambivalent in their use of parody than I had allowed. I want to conclude this chapter by suggesting that it is not simply a matter of two alternative kinds of novel which have been written in Europe since the sixteenth century. Rather, I want to suggest the inclusiveness of the novel as a form, and the mobility and flexibility of parody both within and in relation to it. If we take seriously the contention that novels emerge from the linguistic and discursive competition of heteroglot societies, then we must recognise also the myriad possibilities for parody, and the diverse evaluative attitudes, that the form provides. Our responsibility, then, is perhaps not so much to trace alternative traditions, as to be alert to the diverse ways in which the words of another are celebrated, betrayed, assaulted, ironised, and set in motion in the words of particular and specific novels.

Dickens's novels exemplify these multiple possibilities, in the diverse parodic practices that characterise them. The extraordinary linguistic variety of nineteenth-century England flows through his novels, inflected in many different directions. On occasions the parody is straightforwardly hostile: ' "We Englishmen are Very Proud of our Constitution, Sir. It Was Bestowed Upon Us By Providence. No Other Country is so Favoured as This Country" ' (Podsnap in *Our Mutual Friend*). Elsewhere it is, to use the sentimental word, 'affectionate': ' "There's wonders in the deep, my pretty. Think on it when the winds is roaring and the waves is rowling. Think on it when the stormy nights is so pitch dark ... as you can't see you hand afore you" ' (Captain Cuttle in *Dombey and Son*). On yet other occasions, as I suggested in Chapter 1, Dickens's prose moves into and out of the myriad accents of nineteenth-century London, indicating their presence by no more than a lightly suggested cliché or a turn of phrase. His practice as a novelist suggests both the inevitability of parody in the novel, and the range of uses to which it can be put.

This account of Dickens's writing is partly informed by one emphasis of Mikhail Bakhtin's, which stresses the emergence of the novel as a genre from the heteroglossic variety of complex social orders. It is a moot point how that emphasis can be squared with another account that he gives of one tradition within the novel, in which novels such as those of Dostoevsky are described as 'dialogic'; that is, in the double-voiced words of the text can be heard an engagement of author and character in which the author does not claim ultimate authority for his own point of view. Parody is a typical mode of double-voicing, but it is not necessarily dialogic in this specific sense. Indeed, in so far as parody is simply mocking or dismissive, it might be thought to be the very opposite of dialogic, since it claims for itself the right to destroy the word of the other. But just as parody need not refer to one moment only in the gamut of linguistic interactions, it is important not to sentimentalise Bakhtin either, and make the 'dialogic' exclude some of the more bracing tones that some forms of parody certainly include. So we can conclude, in a manner that recognises the great variety of novelistic practice, that parody is certainly a mode that confronts the word of the author with those of the characters, understood in the widest sense as those whose language enters into the novel, however briefly. But this confrontation can occur in many different ways, and can suggest an equally diverse range of attitudes, not all of which will be ethically benign or dialogic in the manner that Bakhtin imputes to Dostoevsky.

In his parodic dedication to the Fifth Book, 'Treating of the Heroic Deeds and Saying of the Good Pantagruel', Rabelais concludes by comparing the offer of a book to read to the prospect of a dish of beans:

> Then be sure all you that take care not to die of the pip, be sure I say, you take my advice, and stock yourselves with good store of such books, as soon as you meet with them at the booksellers; and do not only shell those beans, but even swallow them down like an opiate cordial, and let them be in you; I say, let them be within you: then you shall find, my beloved, what good they do to all clever shellers of beans.

> (Rabelais, n.d.: 540)

Reading, here, is likened to the digestive process; but we also ought to consider *writing* to be like the digestive process, which ingests the word of another and transforms it. In this context, parody is one of the most important transformative processes. But we all know the peculiar digestive characteristics of the consumption of beans, and perhaps parody is indeed best likened to ... blowing a raspberry!

4

PARODY AND POETRY

The previous chapter demonstrated the pervasiveness of parody both on the borders of the novel and, more importantly, within it. It is doubtful whether parody operates in this latter way in poetry, however, except in the case of such especially 'novelised' poems such as Byron's *Don Juan* (1819–24) and Ezra Pound's *Cantos* (1930–60), where the poems draw upon the multiple registers, styles and jargons of the contemporary world. Rather, in this chapter we shall see how parody has been used extensively in establishing and defending canons of poetic decorum, above all when such canons have appeared to be under threat – at the beginning of the eighteenth century, for example, and again at the century's end. But we shall also have occasion to recognise, again, the productiveness of parody; that is, that the very act of writing parody involves writers in the relativisation of literary languages which it is sometimes their express purpose to combat. The more writers mock the 'bad' poetry of others by means of parody, the more they contribute to the very proliferation of competing styles: just the situation that they seek to resist. This paradox will be especially apparent in the ensuing discussion of neoclassical and, particularly, Scriblerian parodic practices – Scriblerian being the name for the group of writers gathered around Alexander Pope and Jonathan Swift in the early eighteenth century, who shared a set of broadly conservative cultural and political attitudes.

However, it may be that in describing the function of parody as 'establishing and defending canons of poetic decorum', I have given an unduly solemn account of it. It is certainly the case that parody is a weapon in the culture wars of the seventeenth, eighteenth and nineteenth centuries, and I shall be devoting much of this chapter to establishing this point. But I hope also not to forget its playful role, where what is produced by parody is not 'correction' – the recognition of poetic faults and their avoidance in future writing – but more simply delight, be it in the parodist's virtuosity, or the breakdown of poetry into the nonsense which skirts all discourse. Certainly 'nonsense verse' relies heavily upon parody, and it is with this mode of writing that the chapter begins.

In the seventeenth century, according to Noel Malcolm, 'nonsense writing was thought of primarily in terms of a parodic stylistic exercise: to write nonsense was not to express the strangeness of unconscious thought but to engage in a highly self-conscious stylistic game'.[1] The parody to which Malcolm refers here is the parody of fustian or bombast, both in prose and in the dramatic writing of, especially, the playwright Christopher Marlowe (1564–93). In the following chapter I shall consider the role of parody in the theatre, where a whole tradition of burlesque plays has taken the big languages of heroic drama and of melodrama as their targets. Here the point is that for certain seventeenth-century writers, especially the so-called 'Water-poet' John Taylor, the grand diction of Marlowe ('Marlowe's mighty line') became the opportunity to produce parody that inflected the poetry towards nonsense, and where it is hard to see any substantial ideological point at issue. In this respect, as we shall see, this kind of parody differs from the self-consciously serious issues which Ben Jonson (1572–1637), for example, thought to be at stake in the parodies produced in the so-called 'War of the Theatres'. At all events, here are some lines from Marlowe, followed by some of Taylor's nonsense:

> Black is the beauty of the brightest day;
> The golden ball of heaven's eternal fire,
> That danc'd with glory on the silver waves,
> Now wants the fuel that inflam'd his beams,
> And all with faintness and with foul disgrace,
> He binds his temples with a frowning cloud,
> Ready to darken earth with endless night.
>
> (Marlowe, 1969: 98)

Taylor's poem, 'The Essence of Nonsence upon Sence', reads thus:

> Mount meekly low, on blew presumptuous wings,
> Relate the force of fiery water Springs,
> Tell how the Artick and Antartick Pole
> Together met at Hockley in the Hole:
> How Etna, and Vessuvius, in cold bloud,
> Were both drown'd in the Adriatick floud.
> Speak truth (like a Diurnall) let thy Pen
> Camelion like, rouze Lions from their Den,
> Turne frantick Wolpacks into melting Rocks,
> And put Olympus in a Tinder box:
> Report how Ruffian Cats doe barke like dogs,
> And Scithian mountains are turned Irish Bogs,
> Feast Ariadne with Tartarian Tripes,
> Transform great Canons to Tobacco-pipes.
>
> (Malcolm, 1997: 187–8)

Clearly, part of the force of this is to act as a *reductio ad absurdum* of what can appear as the sounding nonsense of Marlowe's verse. The pleasure in Taylor's writing partly derives from lines such as 'Turne frantick Wolpacks into melting Rocks', which reproduces the effects of diction and rhythm that characterise Marlowe's lines, but turns them into brain-defeating nonsense ('Wolpacks', I take it, are literally packs of wool, but I am uncertain if that helps make more sense of the line). However, in opposition to Malcolm, who adopts a strongly anti-Bakhtinian line of argument, it is also possible to recognise in these lines some effects which Bakhtin has taught us to call 'carnivalesque'. That is, some of the pleasure of the poetry derives from the juxtapositions it creates between the 'high' and the 'low', both socially, geographically and physically. Thus when the Artick and the Antartick Poles meet at Hockley in the Hole the effect of bathos derives from the deliberate playing off of the grand against the local and the popular-festive (Hockley in the Hole was a bear-baiting site in Clerkenwell); while Ariadne feasting on Tartarian Tripes is a typically carnivalesque moment, setting in train what can be described in Bakhtinian terms as the swing of grotesque realism in which the play of the upper and lower spheres is set in motion.

Taylor's verse passed into oblivion after the seventeenth century, and indeed it required an act of scholarly recovery by Noel Malcolm to bring back into view the kind of nonsense verse of which he was the most prominent writer. Malcolm himself is keen to stress the learned and scholarly, rather than popular, milieux from which much of this kind of poetry emerged. However, it is not hard to see in the figure of Taylor, who was professionally a Thames waterman, a plebeian outsider who made his bid for poetic fame via a parodic relationship to the grand forms of writing which appear turned upside down in his poetry. In this case, then, it may not be inappropriate to invoke 'carnivalisation' as one context for this early seventeenth-century parodic writing.

However, by the end of the century, and given the triumph of neoclassical notions of writing, it would seem that the policing function of parody became prominent. Certainly Jonathan Swift, Alexander Pope, John Gay, John Arbuthnot (the 'Scriblerians'), and their allies, used parody very centrally in their war on hacks and popular writers, whom they named Dunces and placed in Grub Street. In fact, parody was one of the central weapons that they deployed in the ferocious cultural battles that they fought against what they considered to be the debasement of literature and the betrayal of the whole scholarly–humanist tradition, which they saw themselves as embodying. This is how Pat Rogers, a critic sympathetic to the Scriblerians, describes their enterprise:

> Writers at all times have been conscious of the Grub Street fraternity. That is, major authors – satirists especially – have been aware of a horde of disgruntled literary aspirants baying at their heels: men of slender talent or none at all, racked by envy and embittered by failure. At certain periods this insistent murmur becomes louder, till it almost drowns the voice of the major writer. The early eighteenth century was one such period. We *need* to know something of the lesser fry if we are to understand the procedures or appreciate the rhetoric of the great Augustans. They were all taken up, at a deep level, with the activities of their emulators and detractors. The legend of Grub Street which they did so much to create testifies to the importance that the scribblers had in their mind. Parody, paraphrase, burlesque, mock-encomia, tongue-in-cheek 'answers' – these are the weapons of the Scriblerians. They might also be seen as a kind of devious tribute to Grub Street.
>
> (Rogers, 1980: 175)

In this account, parody is a weapon used in a particular cultural politics, designed to uphold the standards of writing produced by the 'major writer'. Swift's *Tale of a Tub* (1704) or Pope's *The Dunciad* (1728 and 1743) are canonical works for this argument, for they are thick with parodic allusions to the hack writers that they attack.

An immediately accessible example of this Scriblerian parody is provided by the assault on Ambrose Philips (1675–1749), whose pastoral poetry was mocked by Pope and Gay, and whose poetry dedicated to children earned him the nickname 'Namby-Pamby' Philips from the Scriblerian ally Henry Carey (1687?–1743). First, Philips's poem 'To Miss Margaret Pulteney, daughter of Daniel Pulteney Esq; in the Nursery' (1727):

> Dimply damsel, sweetly smiling,
> All caressing, none beguiling,
> Bud of beauty, fairly blowing,
> Every charm to nature owing,
> This and that new thing admiring,
> Much of this and that enquiring,
> Knowledge by degrees attaining,
> Day by day some vertue gaining.
>
> (Philips, 1937)

This provoked Carey to one of the most famous poetic parodies, called 'Namby-Pamby, or, a Panegyric on the New Versification', which begins thus:

> *Naughty Pauty Jack-a-Dandy*
> *Stole a Piece of Sugar-Candy,*
> *From the Grocer's Shoppy-shop,*
> *And away did hoppy-hop.*

And continues:

> Now the venal poet sings
> Baby Clouts, and Baby Things;
> Baby Dolls, and Baby Houses,
> Little Misses, Little Spouses;
> Little Play-Things, little Toys,
> Little Girls, and little Boys.
>
> (Carey, 1729)

The point of this is immediately apparent: Philips is being

accused of writing baby-like verse in order to butter up a potential patron (Pulteney – this is why he's a 'venal' poet). But for all
the pleasure it affords, we should also recognise that this attack is
part of a wider cultural politics which had long ridiculed Philips
for his pastoral poetry, and in which questions of the serious standard of poetry, and anxieties about its professionalisation, are central. While I would scarcely wish to defend Philips's poetry, it
perhaps anticipates the sophisticated simplicities of Wordsworth,
and certainly it is part of a cultural conflict involving issues of
poetic 'primitivism'. Carey, along with the better known mem-
bers of the Scriblerian Club, is thus helping to police the canons
of what counts as permissible in poetry.

However, there is clearly more to be said on the subject of
Scriblerian, and more generally neoclassical, parody, than this
simple account which stresses its function as police weapon on
behalf of high standards. Direct parody of the Carey-on-Philips
kind is in fact only one of a range of more broadly parodic forms
which characterise neoclassical writing, and which include travesty, burlesque, imitation and mock-heroic. All of these forms
rely upon and look back to high-prestige classical writing which,
in principle at least, neoclassical writers seek to transmit forward
into the contemporary world in ways which reproduce and defend
their status. Thus Pope and Gay defend their notions of the pastoral against Philips's debased version of it, while mock-heroic
depends for its effects of comic bathos upon the sad falling-off
from the heroic world to the trivial and contemporary. But in fact
this variety of imitative or second-order forms (which include
parody) testifies to a cultural situation in which the dignities of
classical writing were already compromised. Mock-heroic is a case
in point. While officially this is a form which draws on the prestige of epic to mock the contemporary world – it does not mock
the heroic, but those who fail to be so – potentially at least the mode
surrounds epic forms in destabilising laughter. In fact, the age
failed to produce a successful epic poem; it is highly significant

that both Dryden and Pope wrote very successful translations of classical epics (those of Virgil and Homer successively) but, as far as original poetry is concerned, both produced, characteristically, mock-heroic poems – *MacFleckno* and *The Rape of the Lock*. One way of describing this cultural situation is to say that it was already 'novelised'; that is, it was already in a situation in which the relativisation of discourse had set in and the old hierarchies of genres, with epic and tragedy at the top, had begun to crumble. Parody, in this situation, is almost a condition of writing.

This general description of the cultural situation of the late seventeenth and early eighteenth centuries allows us to reconsider the politics of the Scriblerian group, and to rethink the straightforward assumptions of Pat Rogers as set out above, assumptions that reproduce the Scriblerians' own self-evaluations. Thus another contemporary critic, Brean Hammond, has argued as follows:

> While giving full weight to the very different ways in which it is embodied, I contend that a common cultural politics contours the writing of this group [the Scriblerians]. It derives from a characteristic attitude towards professional writing and the shifting tectonics of patronage, and is elaborated in opposition to a set of literary developments that we can designate under the term 'novelization'. This cultural politics issues in the deployment of parodic literary forms – mock forms, hybrid forms – the common achievement of which is to borrow energy from the sincere forms they wish to explode, and to recycle that energy in subversion.
>
> (Hammond, 1997: 239)

Parodic literary forms, according to this persuasive version of cultural history, are not simply deployed to defend 'major writers' against the hordes of incompetents who are snapping at their heels; rather, they are part of a complex defence of traditional literary hierarchies against the processes of novelisation, which paradoxically draw energies from the very forms they attack.

It may seem odd to use the term novelisation to describe the situation of poetic forms. Perhaps 'relativisation' would better describe the way in which, from the 1660s onwards, a variety of imitative poetic forms came to be pervasive, so that characteristic productions of Restoration poets like Charles Cotton (1630–87), the Earl of Rochester (1648–80) and John Dryden (1631–1700), and their eighteenth-century successors, included travesties, burlesques, imitations, translations, and mock-heroic poems of various kinds. In many cases these poets took their lead from France, where the writers Paul Scarron and Nicolas Boileau had led the way in producing travesty and mock-heroic, though Samuel Butler's *Hudibras* (1663–78) provides an example of a comic-parodic form without parallel in Europe. Thus Cotton, in 1667, published *Scarronides*, a travesty of Virgil written in imitation of Scarron's *Virgile Travestie*. A travesty, according to a now traditional distinction, is the opposite of a mock-heroic; in the former, 'high' matter is treated in a 'low' way, while in the latter, trivial matters are treated in a 'high' or dignified way. Characteristic effects of travesty are those of debasement; of mock-heroic, bathos. Here is the opening of *Scarronides*:

> I Sing the man, (read it who list,
> A *Trojan* true as ever pist)
> Who from *Troy Town*, by wind and weather
> To *Italy*, (and God knows whither)
> Was packt, and wrackt, and lost, and tost,
> And bounc'd from Pillar unto Post.
> Long wandred he through thick and thin;
> Half roasted now; now wet to th'skin;
> By Sea and Land; by Day and Night;
> Forc'd (as 'tis said) by the God's spite:
> Although the wiser sort suppose
> 'Twas by an old Grudge of *Juno*'s,
> A Murrain curry all Curst Wives!

He needs must go, the Devil drives.
                    (Cotton, 1667: 1)

The debasing effects of this are clear enough, achieved by the use
of the plebeian rhyming four-beat line, the colloquialisms, and
the occasional piece of exuberant ribaldry. It has a directly parodic relationship to Virgil's *Aeneid*, which begins '*Arma virumque
cano ...*' ('I sing of arms and of a man ...'); while it is perfectly
possible to imagine this being written in a spirit entirely respectful to Virgil's epic poem, it is also easy to recognise at least some
desacralising impetus or effect here also.

   Imitation, by contrast, might be thought to be the form which
most evidently pays homage to those prestigious forms which it
imitates. It could even be said to be the characteristic form of the
period, as writers attempted their versions of Horace or Juvenal,
Boileau or the Bible, or a hundred other classical, French, Italian
or English poets. Certainly, if we consider the most familiar imitations, such as Pope's Horatian Satires and Epodes (1733–8), or
Johnson's imitation of Juvenal in *London* (1738), we might conclude that the form is marked by deference to its models rather
than any parodic intent with respect to them. However, at times
it is very hard to say where the line between 'imitation' and 'parody' is to be drawn. Considering Pope's extensive youthful imitations, translations and paraphrases, for example, it is difficult to
distinguish those which defer to his poetic models, and those
which appear to mock them. Or consider this 'Imitation' of
Chaucer by Gay, entitled 'An Answer to the Sompner's Prologue
of Chaucer':

   The *Sompner* leudly hath his Prologue told,
   And saine on the Freers his tale japing and bold;
   How that in Helle they searchen near and wide,
   And ne one Freer in all thilke place espyde,
   But lo! the devil turned his erse about,

And twenty thousand Freers wend in and out.
By which in *Jeoffreys* rhyming it appears,
The devil's belly is the hive of Freers.

(Gay, 1926)

Is this parody or imitation? Perhaps it is driven by the opportunity that an imitation of Chaucer provides for some Rabelaisian humour; if it is imitation, it is certainly not motivated by any high opinion of Chaucer as a poet (both Gay and Pope choose to imitate the Chaucer of the comic short tales rather than the romances or *Troilus and Criseyde*). There may be some attempt, in this and in Pope's imitations, to bolster norms of neoclassical decorum by parodying those kinds of poetry which do not measure up – because of their vulgarity, or because of a presumed ignorance of the laws of poetic metre. However, as Gay's example here suggests, imitation may also be a form which permits the presence of energies otherwise excluded from neoclassical verse.

Imitation, then, is a form whose relationship to its models is sometimes ambivalent. The same can be said of mock-heroic, a form which is dense with allusions to high or classical verse, and in which the possibility of parody cannot be excluded. Starting from Boileau's *Le Lutrin* (1674) and Dryden's *MacFleckno* (1682), mock-heroic came to be one of the characteristic forms of the period, including Sir Samuel Garth's *The Dispensary* (1714) and, most famously, *The Rape of the Lock* (1714); more generally, it can be perceived as a tone or generic possibility that is widely used in much of the poetry (and indeed the prose) of the eighteenth century. Is the relationship of this genre towards its classical models as simply deferential as standard accounts would suggest? We could partly answer this by a consideration of two passages by Pope, one from an early version of the translation of Homer, and the next from *The Rape of the Lock*. Sarpedon, a Trojan ally, seeks to encourage the Trojans, and especially Glaucus, in their glorious enterprise:

Why boast we, *Glaucus*, our extended Reign,
Where *Xanthus*' Streams enrich the *Lycian* Plain?
Our num'rous Herds that range each fruitful Field,
And Hills where Vines their Purple Harvest yield?
Our foaming Bowls with gen'rous *Nectar* crown'd,
Our Feasts enhanc'd with Musick's sprightly Sound?
Why on these shores are we with Joy survey'd,
Admir'd as Heroes, and as Gods obey'd?
Unless great Acts superior merit prove,
And vindicate the bounteous Pow'rs above:
'Tis ours, the Dignity They give, to grace;
The first in Valour, as the first in Place:
That while with wondring Eyes our Martial Bands
Behold our Deeds transcending our Commands,
Such, they may cry, deserve the Sov'reign State,
Whom those that Envy dare not Imitate!
Cou'd all our Care elude the greedy Grave,
Which claims no less the Fearful than the Brave,
For Lust of Fame I should not vainly dare,
In fighting Fields, nor urge thy Soul to War.
But since, alas, ignoble Age must come,
Disease, and Death's inexorable Doom;
The Life which others pay, let Us bestow,
And give to Fame what we to Nature owe;
Brave, tho' we fall; and honour'd, if we live;
Or let us Glory gain, or Glory give!

(Pope, 1968: 61–2)

This is a youthful poet, superbly in command of the medium of the 'heroic couplet', yet still straining to find an idiom in English which would appear as dignified, as lofty, and as inspiring, as he presumes the original to be. Just seven years after writing this translation, Pope parodies these lines in a speech in *The Rape of the*

Lock, when Clarissa seeks to encourage Belinda to compromise her indignation at the loss of her lock of hair:

> Say, why are beauties prais'd and honour'd most,
> The wise Man's Passion, and the vain Man's Toast?
> Why deck'd with all that Land and Sea afford,
> Why Angels call'd, and Angel-like ador'd?
> Why round our Coaches crowd the white-glov'd Beaus,
> Why bows the Side-box from its inmost Rows?
> How vain are all those Glories, all our Pains,
> Unless good Sense preserve what Beauty gains:
> That Men may say, when we the Front-Box grace,
> Behold the first in Virtue as in Face!
> Oh! if to dance all Night, and dress all Day,
> Charm'd the Small-pox, or chas'd old Age away;
> Who would not scorn what Huswife's Cares produce,
> Or who would learn one earthly Thing of Use?
> To patch, nay ogle, might become a Saint,
> Nor could it sure be such a Sin to paint.
> But since, alas! frail beauty must decay,
> Curl'd or uncurl'd, since Locks will turn to grey,
> Since painted, or not painted, all shall fade,
> And she who scorns a Man, must die a Maid;
> What then remains, but well our Pow'r to use,
> And keep good Humour still whate'er we lose?
> And trust me, Dear! good humour can prevail,
> When Airs, and Flights, and Screams, and Scolding fail.
> Beauties in vain their pretty Eyes may roll;
> Charms strike the Sight, but Merit wins the Soul.
>
> (Pope, 1968: 237–8)

Pope's note to this section of the poem explicitly describes it as a 'parody of the speech of Sarpedon to Glaucus in Homer'. Clarissa follows the logic of Sarpedon's speech very closely, systematically translating the honours due to heroes into those paid to beauty, and invoking the prospect of death to insist upon the necessity of good sense where Sarpedon had used it as a spur to glory. The pleasures afforded by the passage in *The Rape of the Lock* include the reader's recognition of the hypotext, and admiration for the poet's virtuosity in turning so brilliantly the Homeric tropes into sage advice for young ladies of court and drawing-room. But while this act of metamorphosis certainly involves no disrespect to the epic poem it transforms, it is an evident act of domestication, making due deference, no doubt, to the original context, but plundering Homer not for heroic but for humorous effect.

Mock-heroic carries within itself, then, an implicit recognition of the unsustainability of undiluted heroics in the contemporary world, and the formal parallels and parodies on which it relies do have some retrospective impact on the models upon which they draw. We can include the form, then, among the symptoms of relativisation, for the multiple parodic and imitative forms of neoclassicism testify to a discursive situation in which the generic hierarchies are in manifest crisis – despite the efforts of the Scriblerians and their allies to bolster them. Indeed, the greater these efforts, and the greater the reliance on parody, the more the hierarchies are undermined.

Parody plays a central role in poetry, then, at a period of perceived cultural crisis, when the guardians of the humanist tradition of arts and learning consider it to be under threat. Later in the eighteenth century, Dr Johnson will occasionally resort to parody to see off threats to the appropriate dignity of poetry, as in his celebrated parody of the low diction of imitations of ballads, made popular by the publication of Percy's *Reliques of Ancient English Poetry* (1765):

> I put my hat upon my head,
> And walked into the Strand;
> And there I met another man,

> Whose hat was in his hand.
>> (Johnson, 1964: 269)

Equally, he could use parody in the other direction, to attack the unthinking use of established poetic diction:

> Hermit hoar, in solemn cell,
> Wearing out life's evening gray,
> Smite thy bosom, sage, and tell,
> What is bliss, and which the way?
>
> Thus I spoke; and speaking sigh'd,
> Scarce repressed the starting tear;
> When the smiling sage replied –
> Come my lad, and drink some beer.
>> (Boswell, 1867: 303)

If it was not for the comic deflation of the last line you might not tell that this was parody. However, these are merely the slightest of Johnson's productions (though the former was sufficiently irritating to Wordsworth to merit discussion in the 'Preface' to *The Lyrical Ballads*); it is not until another period of perceived social, cultural and political crisis, at the end of the eighteenth century and the beginning of the nineteenth century, that parody again begins to become an important feature in poetry. *The Anti-Jacobin* (1798) on the one hand, and *Rejected Addresses* (1812) on the other, are crucial indications of the upheavals caused, in poetry, by the related eruptions of the French Revolution and that fundamental shift in sensibility known retrospectively as Romanticism.

In fact, these publications mark two distinct possibilities for poetic parody in the nineteenth century, and its flowering in the ensuing hundred years or so will be marked by these two broadly different kinds. On the one hand, the poetry of *The Anti-Jacobin* was fiercely partisan, attacking all those poetic (and dramatic) forms which were assumed to be in any way sympathetic to

French revolutionary principles. Thus the writers of the journal, George Canning (1770–1827), John Hookham Frere (1769–1846), and George Ellis (1753–1815) happily pilloried poets and writers of widely differing styles who were at all associated with the revolutionary doctrines of Jacobinism. On the other hand, Horace and James Smith, the authors of *Rejected Addresses* (1812), explicitly rejected any political hostilities in their celebrated collection of parodies, and proposed instead a solely humorous intention – though even here they note the readiness with which stylistic extremes lend themselves to parody, so that an implicit poetic norm is discernible in their writing. The multiple parodies that succeed these two models will fall between these two extremes, offering themselves now as purely ludic, now as corrective, either for stylistic or for ideological reasons.

I have already indicated, in Chapter 1, what Canning and Frere make of Southey. They have no hesitation, equally, in attacking Erasmus Darwin (1731–1802), whose 'Philosophy' made him suspect in the atmosphere of the later 1790s, but whose poetry, however eccentric its topic, was written in a manner quite opposite to that of the early Southey. *The Anti-Jacobin* attack on Darwin's poem *The Loves of the Plants* was called 'The Loves of the Triangles', in which the fundamental poetic absurdity of Darwin's verse is parodied, but only in order to assault the connection between philosophy and revolution. Thus the parody includes such splendid nonsense as this:

> For *me*, ye CISSOIDS, round my temples bend
> Your wandering curves; ye CONCHOIDS extend;
> Let playful PENDULES quick vibration feel,
> While silent CYCLOIDS rests upon her wheel;
> Let HYDROSTATICS, simpering as they go,
> Lead the light Naiads on fantastic toe;
> Let shrill ACOUSTICS tune the tiny lyre;
> With EUCLID sage fair ALGEBRA conspire;

> The obedient pulley strong MECHANICS ply,
> And wanton OPTICS roll the melting eye!
> > (Jerrold and Leonard, 1913: 97–8)

However, the poem also includes the following lines, in which the ideological point of the parody becomes plainer:

> Thus, happy FRANCE! in thy regenerate land,
> Where TASTE with RAPINE saunters hand in hand;
> Where, nursed in seats of innocence and bliss,
> REFORM greets TERROR with fraternal kiss;
> Where mild PHILOSOPHY first taught to scan
> The *wrongs* of Providence and *rights* of MAN:
> Where MEMORY broods o'er FREEDOM'S earlier scene,
> The *Lantern* bright, and brighter *Guillotine*.

> > (ibid.: 101)

(The *Lantern*, of course, was the lamppost from which some victims of the revolutionary crowd were strung up in the first heady days of the French Revolution). Darwin here is attacked as a defender of revolutionary outrages, and his philosophy debunked as subversive and irreligious. The absurdity of the poetry is almost beside the point – any stick to beat the horse – though the virtuosity with which Frere and his co-authors manage to parody it naturally adds flair to the assault.

Canning and Ellis also attacked the contemporary fashion for German tragedy, on the grounds that some of its writers also (Schiller and the young Goethe) were in league with the revolutionary devil, and encouraged immorality under the guise of philosophy. The following song comes from a full-length parody of a German tragedy:

> Whene'er with haggard eyes I view
> > This dungeon that I'm rotting in,
> I think of those companions true

Who studied with me at the U-

    -niversity of Gottingen,

    -niversity of Gottingen.

(*Weeps, and pulls out a blue 'kerchief, with which he wipes his eyes; gazing tenderly at it he proceeds*).

(Trussler, 1969: 335)

The parodists are attacking German tragedy here for its sentimentalism; behind these various attacks lurks a defence of neoclassical standards in the manner of the Scriblerians. However, the targets of these parodic assaults were stylistically very disparate, and really only held together by their common, presumed, sympathy to revolutionary principles. *The Anti-Jacobin* writers were only consistent in attacking their targets with a wit and energy that, naturally, help to carry their assault home.

Horace and James Smith, by contrast with the fundamentally political agenda of Frere, Canning and Ellis, explicitly eschewed political motives in their celebrated volume *Rejected Addresses*, which provided an alternative model for parody to that adopted by *The Anti-Jacobin*. This is how they described their aims in writing the series of parodies that make up the volume:

> Although aware that their names [those of Rogers and Campbell] would, in the theatrical phrase, have conferred great strength upon our bill, we were reluctantly compelled to forgo them, and to confine ourselves to writers whose style and habit of thought, being more marked and peculiar, was more capable of exaggeration and distortion. To avoid politics and personality, to imitate the turn of mind, as well as the phraseology of our originals, and, at all events, to raise a harmless laugh, were our main objects.

(Jerrold and Leonard, 1913: 396)

Two conclusions are worth drawing from this. First, there clearly *is* a notion of poetic decorum, embodied in the poetry of Rogers and Campbell, at work in the parodies, according to which only those poets who deviate in pronounced ways from this mean can serve as fit subjects for parody. Second, the simply playful ambitions of the parodists are stressed; in this they will form the model for countless poetic parodies in the nineteenth century, who, published in innumerable separate volumes, newspapers or magazines, will rely, like the Smith brothers, on a playful intimacy with the poetic canon that they imitate.

Rejected Addresses included parodies of a substantial list of early nineteenth-century writers, including Wordsworth, Byron, Southey, Thomas Moore, Walter Scott, and Coleridge. Those of Byron and Coleridge are perhaps especially successful; this is the Byron of *Childe Harold*:

> Sated with home, of wife, of children tired,
> The restless soul is driven abroad to roam;
> Sated abroad, all seen, yet nought admired,
> The restless soul is driven to ramble home;
> Sated with both, beneath new Drury's dome
> The fiend Ennui awhile consents to pine.
>
> (Jerrold and Leonard, 1913: 9)

(The reader should know that the fiction of the whole volume is that all these poems are addresses written for the reopening of the Drury Lane Theatre, submitted to but rejected by the committee which held a competition to decide upon the opening address.) And Coleridge appears in the following guise; his 'Playhouse Musings' include this meditation upon the manner in which the builders work upon the new theatre:

> From that hour,
> As leisure offer'd, close to Mr. Spring's
> Box-office door, I've stood and eyed the builders.
> They had a plan to render less their labours;
> Workmen in olden times would mount a ladder

With hodded heads, but these stretch'd forth a pole
From the wall's pinnacle, they placed a pulley
Athwart the pole, a rope athwart the pulley;
To this a basket dangled; mortar and bricks
Thus freighted, swung securely to the top,
And in the empty basket workmen twain
Precipitate, unhurt, accosted earth.

(ibid.: 50)

This nicely captures some of Coleridge's stylistic habits, including some of the affectations of his diction ('A sordid solitary
thing/Mid countless brethren with a lonely heart/Through courts
and cities ...' ['Religious Musings']), and the peculiarities of the
way he writes verse. There is also a glance perhaps at Coleridge's
notorious laziness.

The volume as a whole made the fortune of the Smith brothers, and was favourably reviewed in the prestigious *Edinburgh
Review*. This journal was, at the time of publication of *Rejected
Addresses*, at the forefront of debates about the new poetics of the
Romantic poets, famously beginning a review of Wordsworth
with the line 'This will never do'. And this suggests one context
in which to understand the parodies included in the volume:
however innocent the intentions of the authors, they were necessarily engaged in the vigorous contentions over poetic style that
characterised the early nineteenth century. These dissensions, in
turn, were not simply matters of literary style but were bound up
with the deeply divided cultural politics of the period, in which,
for example, Hazlitt could describe Wordsworth, whatever his
explicit political allegiance, as providing a 'levelling Muse'; that
is, Wordsworth's style dignified ordinary lives and therefore had
egalitarian implications almost despite the poet's intentions. The
conservative cultural politics that sees the poetry of Rogers and
Campbell as too limpidly excellent to permit parody, at least
needs to be acknowledged.

The publication of *Rejected Addresses* in 1812 sparked off a small publishing boom in volumes of parody, which included James Hogg's *The Poetic Mirror, or the Living Bards of Great Britain* (1816), and Thomas Hood and J.H. Reynolds's *Odes and Addresses to Great People* (1821). The former is of particular interest as indicating a claim to poetic competence on behalf of a plebeian outsider, the 'Ettrick Shepherd'. But in fact many of the practising poets of the period published parodies, including Southey, Byron, and Shelley. Other parodists included Charles Lamb and Thomas Peacock, who was also figured in the previous chapter as the author of the comic symposia *Crotchet Castle* and *Headlong Hall*. Their various parodies were written with varying degrees of hostility, and with differing ideological agendas (or none at all). In short, they make up part of the competitive to-and-fro of discourses which characterises the nineteenth century, and which can be seen as a further extension of the process of 'novelization' asserted by Brean Hammond, following Bakhtin, to be characteristic of the early eighteenth century. This novelisation describes the situation of poetry as much as it does that of the novel.

It is impossible, then, to ascribe a single function to parody amid this contentious racket of competing voices which surrounds the serious business of poetry in the nineteenth century, and through which some of the debates about poetic style were conducted. It is undoubtedly the case that parody could be used to mock stylistic excess, and thus to preserve a notion of decorum; Browning's extravagances provided many opportunities here, as in the following famous assault called 'The Cock and the Bull':

> You see this pebble-stone? It's a thing I bought
> Of a bit of a chit of a boy i'the mid o' the day –
> I like to dock the smaller parts-o'-speech,
> As we curtail the already cur-tail'd cur
> (You catch the paronomasia, play 'po' words?)

Did, rather, i' the pre-Landseerian days.
Well, to my muttons.

(Calverley, 1904: 219)

But equally parody could be used to mock neoclassical diction
itself, or for reasons of personal grudge-bearing, or to mock the
pretensions of attempts at epic diction, or simply as a convenient
comic handle on a contemporary topic. Parody appeared in the
popular press, and in the comic journals which competed with
each other from the 1830s onwards – *Punch* in particular used
parodies extensively. If in the late seventeenth century it was the
mark of a gentleman that he could toss off an epigram or a love
lyric, in the nineteenth century a comparable badge of accom-
plishment among certain groups of lawyers, journalists, and, naturally, literary people, was the ability to write a parody. They
were published in single-authored volumes, and then in anthologies. This nineteenth-century tradition of parody still provides
the staple of such late twentieth-century anthologies as the *Faber
Book of Nonsense Verse* and *The Faber Book of Parodies*. It persists
also in such forms as *New Statesman* competitions and in the work
of, for example, the poet and parodist Wendy Cope, or such occasional publications as *Poems Not on the Underground; A Parody*,
edited by 'Straphanger' (a reference to the 'Poems on the
Underground' published as posters in the London Tube, where
'straphanging' is forced upon many commuters in the rush hour).

However, it is clear that poetic parody has not been as extensive in the last hundred years as it was in the nineteenth century.
In the final chapter I shall discuss more fully the large question of
the place of parody in contemporary culture; here I can simply
assert that, with the displacement of poetry from cultural centrality, those forms such as parody which depend on some intimate
acquaintance with it naturally become less prominent also. If the
nineteenth century can be described as thoroughly 'novelised',
then the twentieth century saw the displacement even of the

novel by film and television, where parody is at least as extensive. There is small chance, in this situation, of poetic parody regaining the position it once held.

Nevertheless, the course of twentieth-century poetic history in English was marked by dissensions over 'style' as emphatic as those of the preceding century. It was noted in Chapter 1 how the battles over Modernism were in part fought out through parody, with Pound's comic assault on 'The Lake Isle of Innisfree' (see p. 35) marking one ground-clearing exercise for the new aesthetic. Equally the stylistic extremes of Modernist poetry provoked a series of parodies, executed with varying degrees of hostility. T.S. Eliot has been one persistent victim of such assaults, given the iconic status of *The Waste Land* (1922) as the quintessential Modernist poem. In the following sequence of parodies, Eliot's poetry is adversely imitated from different directions. First, Henry Reed assaults the Eliot of *The Four Quartets*, in 'Chard Whitlow (Mr. Eliot's Sunday Evening Postscript)':

> As we get older we do not get any younger.
> Seasons return, and to-day I am fifty-five,
> And this time last year I was fifty-four,
> And this time next year I shall be sixty-two.
> And I cannot say I should care (to speak for myself)
> To see my time over again – if you can call it time,
> Fidgeting uneasily under a draughty stair,
> Or counting sleepless nights in the crowded Tube.
>
> (Grigson, 1979: 283)

Here the object of Reed's attack is the manner in which Eliot, in 'Burnt Norton' or 'Little Giddings', teeters on the edge of both prosiness and pomposity; Reed, in fact, seeks to push him over, making Eliot's carefully constructed distinctions sound like fussiness and absurdity. The problem with *The Four Quartets*, in this perspective, is perhaps that they are not extreme enough.

By contrast, Bernard Sharratt's parody seeks to inflect the poem in a more political direction; this is the beginning of a line-by-line rewriting of both 'Burnt Norton' and 'East Coker':

> The history that is past and the history that is present
> Will together, we presume, determine the history to come
> And those histories are always before us.
> For to be fixed in a permanent present
> Is only a dead repetition, a fatal denial.
> What might be and what can be
> Are not merely some slight thought in advance
> But practical, difficult, delicate paces before us.
> What might be and what could be
> Stem from determined decisions, from more than decision.
> The calls of the dying stretch out at us
> From brick walls trickling with blood,
> Moments of misery, outrage and upsurge, courage defeated,
> Efforts that failed. Such calls
> Break on us still.
>   Though to what effect
> Stirring the pages in the autumn study –
> A slight breeze on the brow?
>
> (Sharratt, 1984: 170)

Sharratt prefaces this parody with another one, of an editor introducing the results of a competition; it includes the following hope: 'that in any re-reading of the originals, they would be "shadowed" by a memory of their political counterparts' (ibid.: 169). This, I take it, is more a pious than a parodic hope; Sharratt writes out of a sophisticated understanding of literary history, in which he recognises that our sense of the writing of the past is partly formed by the writing of the present (a point made most memorably by T.S. Eliot himself in 'Tradition and the Individual Talent' [1922]). His parody of T.S. Eliot's *Four Quartets*, then, is made as an intervention in contemporary debates about the political function of literature, in a way that seeks to undermine the depoliticised authority that the poems enjoy. It is certainly not comic, but it has a very specific polemical relationship to its hypotext, which makes it a clear, if untypical example of a parody.

Finally, two more traditional parodies from Roger Tagholm and Wendy Cope, which appear in volumes alongside those of other English classics, and which demonstrate the assimilation of Eliot and his stylistic innovations into the poetic canon. First, a parody aimed at the style of the early T.S. Eliot (though Wendy Cope has also written a splendidly irreverent version of *The Waste Land* in five limericks); this is 'A Nursery Rhyme, as it might have been written by T.S. Eliot':

> Because time will not run backwards
> Because time
> Because time will not run
>
> > *Hickory dickory*
>
> In the last minute of the first hour
> I saw the mouse ascend the ancient timepiece,
> Claws whispering like wind in dry hyacinths,
>
> One o'clock
> The street lamp said,
> 'Remark the mouse that races towards the carpet.'
>
> And the unstilled wheel still turning
> > *Hickory dickory*
> > *Hickory dickory*
>
> *dock*
>
> > (Cope, 1986; 19)

This is parody in playful mode, where the sense of mock-solemnity conveyed upon the nursery rhyme does little to disturb the genuine sense of urgency that can be found in, for example,

'Gerontion' or 'Preludes'. Indeed, the parody here demonstrates the success of the idiom that Eliot fashioned for himself at the beginning of the twentieth century. By way of contrast, here is a less accomplished piece of writing, but one which is centrally in the tradition of nineteenth-century literary parody – 'from *The Waste Land*', by Roger Tagholm:

> April is the cruellest month, bringing
> The tax man out of his dead office,
> Ruining salaries and bonuses, drenching
> Our balances with a rain of demands.
>
> On Moorgate station
> I can connect
> Nothing with nothing
> For that is all that is usually left.
> I have measured out my life in Tax
> Returns:
> This how the world ends
> Not with a bang but an overdraft.
>
> (Tagholm, 1996: 34)

Here, the pleasure of the parody (such as it is) derives from the links that the poet can create between the world of the hypotext and contemporary London – indeed, the City itself. Thus, April becomes the cruellest month not because it 'breeds lilacs out of the dead ground', but because it is the beginning of the new tax year – and so on. In producing these comic connections, the parody is repeating the work done by *The Waste Land* in juxtaposing a prestigious poetic past with a degraded contemporaneity. The original poem, already partly parodic in its relation to earlier poems, itself joins the chain of parodied utterances which it initiated. However, the simply comic intentions of Tagholm as a parodist are quite different from the critical ambitions that mark the original poem.

Parody for the Scriblerians and the anti-Jacobins, we have seen, was an important weapon in a sometimes ferocious cultural politics. The notion of parody handed down to the early twenty-first century, however, derives more from the playful parodies of *Rejected Addresses*; even this richly cacophonous tradition, however, has dwindled to little more than a parlour-game. As we shall see in the following chapter, the history of parody in the theatre at first closely parallels that in poetry, only to diverge quite markedly in the nineteenth century as the popular status of the two arts swerved apart. This large question of the popular context in which parody flourishes – or fails to – is one that provides the substantial topic for the final chapter of this book.

5

THE BEAUTIES OF BURLESQUE

Parody, we have seen, is a word that comes down to us from the ancient Greeks. Burlesque, by contrast, is a seventeenth-century coinage, first used in Italian and then French, but passing rapidly into English. It designated writing both in the theatre and poetry; Scarron's *Virgile Travesti* (1648–52) was described as a burlesque (see p. 104). However, I intend to use the word burlesque to describe a tradition of parodic theatre which runs from the late seventeenth right through to the twentieth century. In doing so I am not of course excluding the use of burlesque as a term for kinds of parodic poetry; I am simply following usage in the theatre itself, where burlesque is the favoured term, and indeed where, in the nineteenth and twentieth centuries, the term has come to have some very specialised uses. Earlier, however, burlesque drama means something very specific: it takes other drama as its topic, for comic effect, relying throughout on local parodies. The tradition is initiated by Buckingham's assault on heroic tragedy in *The Rehearsal* (1671); however, the richly heteroglossic world of the Elizabethan and Jacobean theatre is also shot through with multiple parodies, for various purposes, and no understanding of the place of parody in the theatre would be complete without some consideration of this remarkable moment.

PARODY ON THE ELIZABETHAN AND JACOBEAN STAGE

In the final Act of *Hamlet*, the young Osric is sent to the Prince to bear a challenge from Laertes for a fencing-match, on which Claudius has laid a substantial wager. It is a moment of high drama; Laertes is embittered at Hamlet, and Claudius is fearful of him, because his life is at risk. Yet Shakespeare takes the opportunity to mock a certain kind of highly elaborate and Latinate English; when Osric addresses Hamlet, he replies in kind:

OSRIC: Sir, here is newly come to court Laertes; believe me, an absolute gentleman, full of most excellent differences, of very soft society and great showing. Indeed, to speak feelingly of him, he is the card or calendar of gentry, for you shall find in him the continent of what part a gentleman would see.

HAMLET: Sir, his definement suffers no perdition in you; though, I know, to divide him inventorially would dozy th'arithmetic of memory, and yet but yaw neither in respect of his quick sail. But, in the verity of extolment, I take him to be a soul of great article, and his infusion of such dearth and rareness as, to make true diction of him, his semblable is his mirror, and who else would trace him, his umbrage, nothing more.

(Act V, sc. ii)

You might think that Hamlet is a little unfair here; with scarcely a hint from Osric he is off into a wonderful flight of fancy, in which his diction almost breaks down into nonsense. Unjust or not, this is an exemplary parodic interchange; Hamlet responds to the mild foolishness of Osric's speech with full-blown mockery of it, in which the Latinate abstractions and the elegant metaphors are exaggerated to breaking point. Beyond the specifics of this interchange, there is perhaps a parody here of the notorious elaborations of an Elizabethan prose style pioneered by Lyly in *Euphues* (1578–80).

This example is drawn from one of Shakespeare's tragedies; even here, in the climactic scenes of the drama, the play makes use of a variety of languages, accents and jargons. This is true of Elizabethan and Jacobean theatre more generally, which, while it is certainly capable of high tragic effects, is never hidebound by any notions of tragic decorum, and is throughout characterised by a rich combination of linguistic styles and registers. Parody thrives in such situations, and the plays of the period draw heavily upon it; though in some cases the use of parody is incidental (as here in *Hamlet*), in other instances there is a more structured and systematic use of parody in ways which anticipate the more formal burlesques of a hundred years later.

Despite the remarkable range of dictions available in this period of English drama, it is not surprising that parody thrives most fully in comedy. Jonson's comedies, in a different register to those of Shakespeare, make widespread use of parody to characterise the various obsessions and absurdities that mark out his 'humours' – the psycho-dramatic theory of personality according to which individuals are dominated by particular characteristics. Shakespeare's so-called 'festive comedies', equally, are widely parodic, as different languages are bandied back and forth in the comic exchanges.

The place of parody in one such play, *As You Like It*, can be considered more fully, to give a sense of the pervasiveness of the mode. The jester, Touchstone, parodies lovers' discourse:

> I remember, when I was in love, I broke my sword upon a stone, and bid him take that for coming a-night to Jane Smile; and I remember the kissing of her batler, and the cow's dugs that her pretty chopt hands had milk'd; and I remember the wooing of a peascod instead of her; from whom I took two cods, and, giving her them again, said

with weeping tears 'Wear these for my sake'. We are true lovers run
into strange capers.

(Act 2, sc. iv)

This parody depends on the actor's gesture and intonation as
much as direct verbal mimicry; its satirical object is the absurdities into which lovers run. By contrast, Jaques' parody of the
courtiers' pastoral song in the following scene is more directly
verbal:

> Who doth ambition shun,
> And loves to lie i'the sun,
> Seeking the food he eats,
> And pleas'd with what he gets,
> Come hither, come hither, come hither,
> Here shall he see
> No enemy
> But winter and rough weather.

JAQUES: I'll give you a verse to this note that I made yesterday in despite
of my invention.
AMIENS: And I'll sing it.
JAQUES: Thus it goes:

> If it do come to pass
> That any man turn ass,
> Leaving his wealth and ease
> A stubborn will to please,
> Ducdame, ducdame, ducdame;
> Here shall he see
> Gross fools as he,
> An if he will come to me.

(Act 2, sc. v)

This has the structure of a riposte or 'reply' poem; the invitation to a pastoral life in the courtiers' song is directly answered by Jaques's parody of it, though the exact force of the parody is somewhat mysterious, especially given the uncertainty of the meaning of 'ducdame'. There is a similar riposte structure to Touchstone's parody of Orlando's love poetry in Act 3; Orlando has pinned his verse to trees all over the forest, and Rosalind has found them:

ROSALINDE: From the east to western Inde,
No jewel is like Rosalinde.
Her worth, being mounted on the wind,
Through all the world bears Rosalinde.
All the pictures fairest lin'd
Are but black to Rosalinde.
Let no face be kept in minde
But the fair of Rosalinde.

TOUCHSTONE: I'll rhyme you so eight years together, dinners, and suppers, and sleeping hours excepted. It is the right butter-women's rank to market.

ROSALINDE: Out, fool!

TOUCHSTONE: For a taste:
If a hart do lack a hind,
Let him seek out Rosalinde.
If the cat will after kind,
So be sure will Rosalinde.
Winter garments must be lin'd,
So must slender Rosalinde.
They that reap must sheaf and bind,
Then to cart with Rosalinde.
Sweetest nut hath sourest rind,
Such a nut is Rosalinde.
He that sweetest rose will find
Must find love's prick and Rosalinde.

(Act 3, sc. ii)

Touchstone indeed describes Orlando's poetry as 'the very gallop of false verses'. The humour here is simple and immediate, not to say mildly obscene; its victim is not only Orlando's bad poetry but also the very hyperbolic language in which love poetry is cast.

In the two parodies by Touchstone we can see a kind of comic degrading of the high language of love, while Jaques' target is the discourse of courtly pastoral. The social and cultural origins of these comic degradings are widely different; Touchstone comes from the tradition of popular foolery, while Jaques is a mouthpiece for a more learned 'melancholy' tradition. Neither voice can be thought of as normative; *As You Like It*, like most of Shakespeare's comedies, is made up of a rich texture of diverse languages, both verse and prose, between which there are many complex interchanges, and none of which is endowed with any final authority.

Parody is still more pervasive in *Love's Labour's Lost*, though in the case of this earlier play the element of learned fun – or fun at the expense of the learned – is more prominent. The play consists of innumerable parodies of courtly language, of the hyperboles and far-fetched similes of love poetry, and of an extraordinary style of discourse described thus by Berowne:

> Taffeta phrases, silken terms precise,
> Three-pil'd hyperboles, spruce affectation,
> Figures pedantical.

> (Act 5, sc. ii)

But as with *As You Like It*, there is no normative notion here against which this 'deviant' or exaggerated speech can be measured. The languages of learned fools like Holofernes and Sir Nathaniel are also parodied; after a meal together they erupt onto the stage in a wonderful gabble of cod Latin and affected English; in the words of the page boy Moth, 'they have been at a great feast of languages, and stol'n the scraps' (Act 5, sc. ii). This could stand as an excellent description of the play itself; it is a 'feast of languages', and parody is one of the means by which the audience is made aware of the multiple vocabularies from which the various dishes are made.

These two Shakespearean comedies, then, offer examples of a way of writing plays which can genuinely be described as 'carnivalesque'; that is, it draws upon a variety of accents and vocabularies, subjects them all to complex cross-exchanges, and makes the 'high' languages of courtesy, love and pastoral (among others) the topic for a bracing laughter. But this is certainly not the only manner of play-writing to use parody widely in the early seventeenth century. The comedies of Ben Jonson use the mode in a way which is arguably more normative, especially in *The Poetaster* (1601), a play written as part of the so-called 'poetomachia' (or battle of the poets) when Jonson on the one side, and Marston and Dekker on the other, engaged in prolonged dispute about the appropriate language and style for drama. This gave Jonson the opportunity for numerous parodies of his opponents, as in this brief assault upon Marston:

> Where art thou, boy? Where is Calipolis?
> Fight earthquakes in the entrails of the earth,
> And eastern whirlwinds in the hellish shades;
> Some foul contagion of the infected heavens
> Blast all the trees, and in their cursed tops
> The dismal night raven and tragic owl
> Breed and become forerunners of my fall.
>   (Jonson, 1967: I, 265; Act III, sc. i)

The target of Jonson's parody here is what he sees as Marston's bombast, the style of writing that was the starting-point, also, of the tradition of seventeenth-century nonsense poetry discussed in the previous chapter. Elsewhere in the play Jonson attacks other styles of play-writing, including the 'alliterative and solemn style' (Clinton-Baddeley, 1952: 17) of earlier Elizabethan drama. His regulatory ambitions are clear, and are spelt out in the last scene of the play, when Virgil (the play is set in classical Rome) is brought on to make the moral plain. Jonson casts himself as the authoritative Horace; in the following quotation, for 'Gallo-Belgic' read 'French':

> You must not hunt for wild outlandish terms,
> To stuff out a peculiar dialect;
> But let your matter run before your words.
> And if at any time you chance to meet
> Some Gallo-Belgic phrase, you shall not straight
> Rack your poor verse to give it entertainment,
> But let it pass.
>
> (Jonson, 1967: I, 297; Act V, sc. i)

'Let your matter run before your words'; this is a classic statement of a normative view of language, in which subject-matter precedes the discourse which clothes it. Any exaggerations of discourse, any deviations from the plain and straightforward way of saying things dictated by the matter itself, are deemed fit topics for parody.

However, the wonderfully inventive gusto with which Jonson imitates and parodies the hundred and one jargons of contemporary England in his comedies somewhat belies the would-be authoritative position adopted at the end of *The Poetaster*, which is marked by the immediate polemical purposes of his dispute with Marston and Dekker. In *Volpone*, *The Silent Woman*, *The Alchemist* or *Bartholomew Fair*, for example, Jonson lampoons the language of politicians, alchemists, and Puritans, imitates the cant of thieves and bawds, and generally allows the multiple voices of early seventeenth-century London so thoroughly into his plays that they defeat the regulative intentions that seek to control them. In *Bartholomew Fair* (1614), especially, the delight in the various slangs and jargons that run through the fair perhaps draws some of its energy from the great popular festival which the play dramatises, and scarcely suggests any norm or standard against which these diverse languages are to be measured.

A further aspect of Jonson's comedies lends itself to the formally self-conscious or metafictional moment of parody, namely his frequent use of elaborate inductions, prologues, and afterwords to establish the credentials of his writing and to hold them up as in some way exemplary. His practice in this respect deserves the coinage 'metadramatic', and is close to that of the 'play within a play' structure to which the burlesque tradition is drawn; the form naturally lends itself to burlesque since it allows the dramatist to display the stigmatised style or genre in a relatively secure way. The possibilities of this construction are famously exploited by Shakespeare also, in the 'tedious brief scene' of Pyramus and Thisbe in *A Midsummer Night's Dream* (1595); but they are used to equally good effect in Beaumont and Fletcher's *The Knight of the Burning Pestle* (1613). Shakespeare's target is similar to one of Jonson's in *The Poetaster*, namely the old alliterative drama:

> Sweet moon, I thank thee for thy sunny beams;
> I thank thee, Moon, for shining now so bright;
> For, by thy gracious, golden, glittering gleams,
> I trust to take of truest Thisbe sight.
>> But stay, O spite!
>> But mark, poor knight,
> What dreadful dole is here!
>> Eyes do you see?
>> How can it be?
> Oh dainty duck! Oh dear!

> (Act 5, sc. i)

The parody here, however, is complicated by the social dynamics in which it is located. The play is being performed by the workmen of Athens for the entertainment of their betters, who interrupt the performance with a series of insulting remarks. At first sight this would appear to align the old and stigmatised form with working-class naïveté and ignorance, and the romantic comedy which surrounds it with aristocratic sophistication. However, it is not clear that the current of the audience's sympathies need run simply with the wit of the aristocratic mockers and against the evident good will of the performers, and, in the ambience of good feeling generated by the performance of the play within the play, the parody of the simple old form can appear affectionate. Indeed, depending upon performance style and audience disposition, it may be that the story of Pyramus and Thisbe retains its continuing power to move.

The Knight of the Burning Pestle uses the 'play within a play' to different effect. In a Jonsonian Induction scene, a Citizen and his wife are established as having theatrical ambitions for their son Ralph, who, they insist, must take the leading role in the play; they continually interrupt the performance when they are dissatisfied with his role. Ralph gets to play the role of the Knight of the Burning Pestle; in a manner that explicitly recalls Cervantes, the comedy depends upon the notion of a modern apothecary's son imagining himself in a world of knight-errantry. This permits numerous incidental parodies within the general burlesque framework, as in the following Quixote-like moment when Ralph approaches the tapster of the Bell Inn in Waltham Forest as though he were the squire of a holy and hospitable order:

RALPH: Fair Squire Tapstero! I, a wandering knight,
        Hight of the Burning Pestle, in the quest
        Of this fair lady's casket and wrought purse,
        Losing myself in this vast wilderness,
        Am to this castle well by fortune brought,

Where, hearing of the goodly entertain
Your knight of holy order of the Bell
Gives to all the damsels, and all errant-knights,
I thought to knock, and now am bold to enter.
                    (Beaumont and Fletcher, 1875: 301)

This displays the true Cervantian distance between the parodied discourse and the prosaic facts of the ordinary world, compounded by the obscene potential of the title phrase itself. But this is by no means the only element of parody in the play, for Ralph gets to play a variety of roles, and his enthusiastic acting of them points at a number of satiric targets: the old English folk drama ('And by the common counsel of my fellows in the Strand/With gilded staff and crossed scarf the May-lord here I stand'); the would-be soldierly talk of the City trained-bands ('March fair, my hearts! Lieutenant, beat the rear up. Ancient, let your colours fly; but have a great care of the butchers' hooks at Whitechapel'); perhaps even the speech of Shakespearean history plays. Other parts of the play also parody the conventions of contemporary drama.

The Knight of the Burning Pestle is one precursor of the tradition of burlesque drama that begins in the Restoration theatre. However, its linguistic variety, and its commingling of various languages and dialects, mark it out as a clear contemporary of Jonson and Shakespeare. It is perhaps not an accident that burlesque should become a recognised and popular genre of drama on the Restoration stage, marked by much greater linguistic decorum than theatre earlier in the century, since the energies of burlesque now have to be channelled into a specific genre and cannot find expression in the more carefully policed neoclassical genres. On the other hand, the linguistic refinement of Restoration comedy should not be exaggerated; Etherege's language in *The Man of Mode* (1676) was sufficiently coarse to shock Richard Steele thirty years later. However, the 1670s was certainly the

decade of *The Rehearsal*, which inaugurates the tradition of burlesque theatre properly so called.

BURLESQUE DRAMA

If the obvious parallel and inspiration for *The Knight of the
Burning Pestle* is *Don Quixote*, then the clear analogue for the tradition of burlesque theatre in the Restoration and the eighteenth
century is provided by the battles over heroic poetry. The main
targets of these burlesque plays are the excesses of heroic tragedy;
it is clear that some of the same cultural battles are being fought
out here as dominate the writing of poetry in the same period.
The critic Claude Rawson makes the connection in this way:

> Part of the epic impulse, adulterated by romance elements and gener-
> ally coarsened, was diverted, by Dryden and others, into the heroic
> play, a genre which was quickly seen by many as a further example of
> the failure of the heroic mode to animate genuinely good writing. It
> became a target for parody from *The Rehearsal* to Fielding's *Tragedy
> of Tragedies*, much as many modern epics were parodied and derided.
>
> (Rawson, 1985: 203)

We can generalise this comment to indicate the wider crisis of
confidence over epic as a mode that characterises the period;
whereas in poetry this manifests itself in travesty and mock-
heroic, in the theatre it produces the burlesque.

This suggests a question, however, about the nature of the
satiric target of these burlesques. In discussing mock-heroic, it
was noted that while the genre was notionally deferential to the
epic poetry that it parodied, it nevertheless indicated considerable
uncertainties about that high-prestige form. Burlesque theatre,
by contrast, has generally been construed as straightforwardly
hostile to heroic theatre, rather than to its 'excesses', as in the phrase
I used above. The tragic actor Quin, famous for his declamatory

style, is said to have remarked on Henry Carey's burlesque *Chrononhotonthologos* (1734) that 'if the young fellow is right, we are all in the wrong' – though the remark is also said to have been directed at Garrick.[1] It may even be that the burlesques contributed to the death of heroic tragedy as such; on the other hand, such tragedies persisted in the repertoire of the English theatre during the whole period when burlesques were most popular. On the other hand again, it is also striking that the parodic form continued to be written and performed long after the heroic plays that they attacked had ceased to enjoy any theatrical currency. Indeed, some of the jokes pioneered in early eighteenth-century burlesque theatre persist in contemporary pantomime when the form which they originally parodied has been dead for over two centuries. At all events, burlesque at the very least undermined the legitimacy of the heroic drama it parodied, and testifies to a widespread uncertainty about the possibility of heroic elevation in the late seventeenth and early eighteenth centuries. This ambivalence about the target of the parody – is it the genre, or only bad examples of the genre? – will be at the centre of the burlesque throughout its history.

The paradox of parody is certainly evident in these plays. In attacking one form, the writers of burlesque have succeeded in creating another that only exists by virtue of its antagonistic relationship to the genre they wish to mock. One of the principal historians of the genre, V.C. Clinton-Baddeley, considers its strength to be that it achieves a humour which is beyond the immediate antipathies of mere travesty or direct parody; certainly, in considering the burlesques of Henry Carey, such as *Chrononhotonthologos* and *The Dragon of Wantley* (1737), or Henry Fielding's *Tom Thumb* (1730), we can recognise that the playwrights strike a vein of extravagant humour which takes the genre well beyond merely negative critique. This certainly accounts for the persistence of these plays long after their original targets were forgotten. In this respect, these later burlesques have moved on considerably from their generic model, Buckingham's *The Rehearsal* (1671).

This play uses the play-within-a-play construction to attack contemporary heroic tragedies, including those of Davenant and, especially, Dryden, who figures in the play as the playwright Bayes. Doubtless individual rivalries also played a part in Buckingham's burlesque, since Dryden and Buckingham were opposed on many literary and political matters. But there is no doubting the *corrective* function of the parody; indeed, it may have contributed to Dryden's abandonment of heroic tragedy. The play consists of scraps of the parodied play, notionally in rehearsal, intercut with a running commentary from a pair of hostile critics, and the defence offered by the author, Bayes. The play's target is not heroic elevation as such but the incoherence with which heroic plays drag in elements of the heroic tradition, as in the following parody of the epic simile:

CLORIS: As some tall Pine, which we, on Æ'tna find
             T'have stood the rage of many a boist'rous wind,
             Feeling without, that flames within do play,
             Which would consume his Root and Sap away;
             He spreads his woorsted Arms unto the Skies,
             Silently grieves, all pale, repines and dies:
             So, shrowded up, your bright eye disappears.
             Break forth, bright scorching Sun, and dry my tears.
             [*Exit.*]
JOHNSON: Mr. *Bayes*, Methinks this *simile* wants a little application too.
BAYES: No faith; for it alludes to passion, to consuming, to dying,
             and all that; which, you know, are the natural effects of an
             Amour.

                                                              (Trussler, 1969: 20)

The parodic epic simile will be a staple of the burlesque theatre for the next 150 years. Here, in case there should be any doubt about the point of the parody, the critic Johnson is on hand to point the moral, while Bayes can defend himself with a suitably ludicrous reply. There is clearly a strongly regulatory aspect to the play here, as throughout it seeks to expose the absurdities of the genre that it mocks; yet it is never clear whether there is an unambiguously excellent model of heroic tragedy by which the deficiencies of the parodied examples can be measured.

John Gay's two burlesques, *The What D'Ye Call It* (1715) and *Three Hours After Marriage* (1717), are perhaps less ambivalent; but then their parodic object is not heroic tragedy. The former's sub-title, 'A Tragi-Comi-Pastoral Farce', sufficiently indicates its target: the general mingling of genres in an all-purpose tragicomedy, characteristic of Addisonian drama.[2] *The What D'Ye Call It* retains the play-within-a-play structure of *The Rehearsal*, but manages also some elaborate interplay between the levels of the fiction. The hybrid nature of the target permits a variety of parodies, of sentimental pastoral, of ballads, and of moralised 'happy endings'. This latter target will reappear in Gay's most famous play, *The Beggar's Opera* (1728), which, while not strictly a burlesque, has many strongly parodic elements in it, especially of the very theatrical conventions on which many plays depend. Here is one of the parodies from *The What D'Ye Call It*; the heroine of the play is apostrophising her rake in sentimental fashion:

KITTY: Dear happy fields, farewell; ye flocks, and you
        Sweet meadows, glitt'ring with the pearly dew:
        And thou, my rake, companion of my cares,
        Giv'n by my mother in my younger years;
        With thee the toils of full eight springs I've known,
        'Tis to thy help I owe this hat and gown;
        On thee I lean'd, forgetful of my work,
        While *Tom* gaz'd on me, propt upon his fork:

> Farewell, farewell; for all thy task is o'er,
> Kitty shall want thy service now no more.
> [*Flings away the rake.*]

(Trussler, 1969: 84)

Gay is evidently caught up here in a similar cultural politics to that driving his contemporary parodies of Ambrose Philips's pastorals; part of the problem with sentimental drama, it seems, is that it is just footling, and in being so it dignifies the minor objects of ordinary lives with an attention they do not deserve. Scriblerian parody, of which this is an example, is based upon a confident set of assumptions about genre, which nevertheless does not prevent the parodic paradox coming into play; in these plays of Gay there is evident an exactly comparable set of attitudes to those of Pope and Swift which were discussed in the previous chapter.

Fielding's parody in *Tom Thumb* (1730; reissued as *The Tragedy of Tragedies* in 1731) works in a similar way, in which the target is ostensibly the debasement of the heroic tradition by the host of contemporary scribblers – indeed, Fielding casts himself as the immediate heir of the Scriblerians, and assumes just the same cultural attitudes. Part of this notional debasement is a result of the abandonment of the rich heritage of classical topics in favour of local and vernacular ones, drawn from the English folk tradition; hence a tragedy based on the figure of Tom Thumb. This provides wonderful opportunities for bathos, exploited fully by Fielding:

KING: *Tom Thumb*! Odzooks, my wide extended Realm
Knows not a Name so glorious as *Tom Thumb*.
Not *Alexander* in his highest Pride,
Could boast of merits greater than *Tom Thumb*.
Not *Caesar*, *Scipio*, all the Flow'rs of *Rome*,
Deserv'd their Triumphs better than *Tom Thumb*.

(Trussler, 1969: 157–8)

But even this brief example displays the instability of the genre, since it is easy to hear in these lines a parody of the usual diction of heroic tragedy, which begins to sound simply like ranting. What starts out as an assault on the debasement of the tradition of tragedy rapidly becomes indistinguishable from laughter at the very possibility of high theatrical seriousness. In the following quotation, Queen Dollalolla is soliloquising on her illicit and secret passion for Tom Thumb:

QUEEN: But hold! – perhaps I may be left a Widow:
         This match prevented, then *Tom Thumb* is mine,
         In that dear Hope, I will forget my Pain.
                   So when some Wench to *Tothill-Bridewell*'s sent,
         With beating Hemp, and Flogging, she's content;
         She hopes, in Time, to ease her present Pain;
         At length is free, and walks the Streets again.

                                                        (Trussler, 1969: 160)

The parodic epic simile is here working in the opposite way to its use in *The Rehearsal*, where it was parodied as a kind of all-purpose indication of high seriousness. In Fielding's hands, the point of the parody is that the simile debases rather than elevates; while this may be aimed at contemporary Grub Street writing, its more general effect is to undermine the pretensions of heroic tragedy to be sealed off from the considerations of the contemporary world, and to level down the anxieties of a tragedy queen to those of a street-walker.

Fielding's burlesques therefore take on a life of their own, independent of their immediate parodic occasion. This is still truer of the burlesques of his contemporary Henry Carey, whose *Chrononhotonthologos* (1734) and *The Dragon of Wantley* (1737) were at least as popular in the theatre as Fielding's burlesques. The very title of the first of these indicates one target of its humour: the outlandish names and topics chosen as the subjects for heroic drama. Indeed, the play is much more straightforwardly a parody of such drama than any of the previous examples, as in the following announcement that the king of the Antipodes has launched an attack on the kingdom:

CAPTAIN: To Arms! To Arms! Great *Chrononhotonthologos*!
           Th'*Antipodean* Pow'rs, from Realms below,
           Have burst the solid Entrails of the Earth.
           Gushing such *Cataracts* of *Forces* forth,
           This World is too incopious to contain 'em:
           Armies, on Armies, march in Form stupendous;
           Not like our Earthly Legions, Rank by Rank,
           But Teer o'er Teer, high pil'd from Earth to Heaven.

                                                    (Trussler, 1969: 220)

The parody of bombast, of heroic hyperbole, and of impressive-sounding foreign names, is evident here; but so is the development of this parody into a vein of fantasy that outlives its immediate occasion. While it would be possible to claim some corrective function for this, the humour that it displays is better understood in the context of a wider crisis of the heroic mode than as a narrowly focused argument about its misdirection in particular contemporary examples.

These burlesque plays and operas of Fielding, Gay and Carey are the most visible and widely imitated of a large number of such productions in the mid- and late eighteenth-century theatre, which provided a rich menu of comic drama, especially comic opera. Traditional comedy (as opposed to the sentimental kind) continued to be written by authors such as Samuel Foote and Arthur Murphy; this inevitably relied largely on parody, as the particular slangs and jargons of comic types and humours were mined for parodic effect. Samuel Foote began his career as a mimic, parodying the styles of other actors; he also pioneered the miscellaneous revue, prominently featuring such imitation. The descendants of this form, in the myriad nineteenth-century burlesque forms such as the burletta, indicate at least some continuities between eighteenth- and nineteenth-century theatre.

Sheridan's *The Critic* (1779) has a more immediately corrective role, and is much nearer to the model of *The Rehearsal* than any of the intervening plays. This is consistent with Sheridan's project of reinventing the strengths of the Restoration stage for the late eighteenth century. Thus *The Critic* re-uses the format of the play-within-a-play, in which a series of critics attend a rehearsal of a new play and pass appropriate remarks upon it, while the dramatist defends it if he can. But the target in this case has changed; it is no longer the genre of seventeenth-century heroic tragedy, but the late eighteenth-century fashion for history plays in the Shakespearean manner, such as Hannah More's *Percy* (1777), or the plays of Richard Cumberland, including *The Battle of Hastings* (1778). In addition, the play attacks another later eighteenth-century genre, the *comédie larmoyante*, or sentimental comedy; Sheridan thus resumes the attack of Gay, earlier in the century, on the generic confusions of English theatre. His targets, in other words, are directly contemporary, a fact reflected in the acting versions of the play which continuously developed over the succeeding one hundred years. But while there are some specific parodies in the play (and others were introduced by the actors), the play works more by general parody, and in it too the parodied verse takes on a life of its own. In the following extract, the Governor of Tilbury is addressing his daughter Tilburina and announces the arrival of the Spanish Armada:

GOVERNOR: How's this – in tears – O Tilburina, shame!
                Is this a time for maudling tenderness,
                And Cupid's baby woes? – hast thou not heard
                That haughty Spain's Pope-consecrated fleet
                Advances to our shores, while England's fate,
                Like a clipp'd guinea, trembles in the scale!

                                  (Sheridan, 1975: 369)

Critics of *The Critic*, like those of mock-heroic with respect to classical epic, have been keen to point out that its target is bad tragedy, not tragedy in general, though a contemporary reviewer of the play thought otherwise: 'Certain, however, it is, that since the exhibition of *The Critic*, tragedy, which a celebrated writer has declared to be one of the greatest exertions of the human mind, is fallen into contempt; it will be some time at least before she can recover the blow' (quoted in Clinton-Baddeley, 1952: 72). Reading these lines from the play, it is also hard to distinguish the parody of eighteenth-century Shakespearean pastiche from downright parody of Shakespeare. The parody, in other words, works by its delight in creating Elizabethan-sounding verse, which teeters pleasantly on the verge of the ludicrous, and threatens to destabilise the whole elaborate tragic edifice.

Nevertheless, despite the opinion of the reviewer just quoted, it is clear that a taste for burlesque and a taste for heroic tragedy, in whatever idiom, could coexist. Sheridan himself displayed no bashfulness about using the idiom of heroic tragedy in his version of Kotzebue's play *Pizarro* (1799). *The Critic* takes an idiom of the contemporary theatre as its parodic target; nevertheless, old-fashioned heroic tragedy continued to be burlesqued despite the disappearance of the genre from the repertoire. William Barnes Rhodes wrote a successful burlesque of this kind in *Bombastes Furioso* (1810), in which many of the same targets – and the same jokes – are repeated ('Hail, Artaxominous! Ycleped the Great!/ I come, a humble pillar of thy state,/Pregnant with news' {Trussler, 1969: 355}); this play continued in the comic repertoire well into the nineteenth century, when the dominant theatrical mode is that of melodrama. This produced its own burlesque; but there is also a tradition of burlesque plays which take Elizabethan theatre as their target, which deserves brief consideration.

There is in fact a very large number of nineteenth-century parodies of Shakespeare, of varying degrees of success. There is also, as a kind of culmination to this tradition, a full-length parody of the Elizabethan verse-play written by George Bernard Shaw, *The Admirable Bashville* (1901), composed, or so he tells us in the Preface, because he had to write the play in a hurry and blank verse is so much easier to write than prose. Like much late nineteenth-century and early twentieth-century parody, the play is there to demonstrate the parodist's virtuosity; its hero, ironically enough for the never-bashful Shaw, is the bashful Bashville himself, whose constancy goes unrewarded. Like much burlesque, much of its humour derives from bathos, the comic distance between manner and topic, helped along by the occasional introduction of a piece of contemporary slang:

LYDIA: My cousin ails, Bashville. Procure some wet.
           [*Exit Bashville.*]
LUCIAN: Some wet!!! Where learnt you that atrocious word?
           This is the language of a flower-girl.
LYDIA: True. It is horrible. Said I 'Some wet'?
           I meant, some drink. Why did I say 'Some wet'?
           I feel as though some hateful thing had stained me.
           Oh Lucian, how could I have said 'Some wet'?

                                               (Shaw, 1937: 1078)

As with so much burlesque, it is impossible to say simply that the humour here works to deflate heroic elevation or to attack modern-day triviality; the humour is certainly capable of working in both directions, sometimes in the same moment. In the quoted example, Lydia's exaggerated horror at being caught out in a vulgarism is nicely exposed by her assumption of tragic tones; while the parody of the tragic tones on this trivial occasion suggests something of the over-inflation of language to which Elizabethan tragedy is liable. It is a delicate balancing act which Shaw sustains remarkably over the three acts of a full-length play.

A later example is to be found in Max Beerbohm's *Savonarola Brown* (1919), though this is really a closet burlesque, since it was never intended to be performed, and is to be placed alongside the prose parodies of *A Christmas Garland*. There is in fact a minor tradition of closet burlesque plays, starting with Canning, Frere and Ellis's *The Rovers* (1799), which forms part of the ferocious cultural politics of *The Anti-Jacobin*. This attacks the sentimentality, louche morals, and ludicrous anachronisms of German tragedy, bundled together as symptoms of the pro-revolutionary malaise. But both these closet burlesques take us away from the cultural politics of the theatre, which is the immediate and most important context for all the burlesque plays that I have discussed. Despite the persistence of many of the tropes of burlesque into contemporary pantomime, there can never really be a flourishing tradition of theatrical parody which is quite divorced from actual and contemporary theatrical practice. This is part of the reason for Sheridan's success in *The Critic*, where he realised that the contemporary mode of Shakespearean pastiche was a more appropriate target than the outmoded heroic tragedy.

The tradition of English burlesque theatre in the Restoration and the eighteenth century cannot simply be explained by its parodic relation to heroic drama. As we have seen, some of the targets of the tradition are the generically mixed sentimental plays of the period, and later there is a further development which takes Elizabethan plays (or at least pastiches of them) as their target. But built into the whole genre are several instabilities, which allow the object of the various parodies to point in differing directions, sometimes against bombast, and at other times against triviality; now against the excesses of the heroic mode, and occasionally throwing the whole possibility of heroic elevation into doubt. While such instabilities prevent any too simple or *a priori* descriptions of the target of burlesque, they also suggest something of the complexities of the eighteenth-century theatre. The nineteenth-century theatre, dominated by melodrama, produced its own and distinctive tradition of burlesque to accompany it.

BURLESQUE MELODRAMA – AND AFTER

In the year after William Barnes Rhodes had his traditional burlesque play, *Bombastes Furioso*, played at the licensed Haymarket theatre in 1810, across the river at the Surrey theatre, in surroundings
that were more legally and socially ambiguous, Dennis Lawler's
play *The Earls of Hammersmith* was performed. The former play
attacked a target that was long dead; the latter was the first of a long
line of parodies of a new theatrical mode, the melodrama. This was a
decidedly popular form, destined to become the dominant mode in
the nineteenth century, which characteristically dramatised the triumph of a threatened moral order via a pictorial dramaturgy – that
is, a way of staging plays which was highly pictorial in its reliance on
gesture and scene-drop. Though *The Earls of Hammersmith, or The
Cellar Spectre, a Comical Tragical Burlesque* retained elements of the
eighteenth-century burlesque tradition, it took the conventions of
the new mode as its target, thus inaugurating a distinctive tradition
in nineteenth-century theatre.

However, it would be a mistake to suggest that burlesque had
the same relationship to melodrama in the nineteenth century as
it had had to heroic tragedy in the eighteenth. Two immediately
complicating factors need to be reckoned in. First, burlesque was
only one of a range of forms in the nineteenth-century theatre
which included more or less of parody, and which assembled and
reassembled a complex variety of specific theatrical practices and
traditions, some already pioneered in the previous century:
burletta, pantomime, and extravaganza all ran alongside burlesque, and included varying elements of direct parody, broad
comedy, topical jokes, musical jokes, dancing girls, acrobatics,
conjuring tricks, equestrianism, pugilism, the occasional balloon
descent, and doubtless many other theatrical or circus-derived
performance styles as well. Second, we must consider the proliferation of theatres and other performance spaces in the nineteenth-
century, which took drama well beyond the confines of the

eighteenth-century licensed theatres. These spaces included just such theatres as the Surrey, which started life as a circus, and continued throughout the nineteenth century to move nearer to, and further from, theatrical legitimacy, as market or management altered. It was one of a large number of suburban theatres, in London and other conurbations, that catered for lower-middle-class and working-class audiences, and provided them with melodramas, burlesques, and the other proliferation of theatrical forms that I have mentioned.

The nineteenth-century theatre, then, was a complex institution, permitting the performance of a wide variety of forms. Though melodrama might eventually become the dominant mode in this theatre, at the beginning of the century it was definitely an upstart form, starting outside the legitimate theatre in both France and England, and only gradually making its way up the escalator of cultural prestige. Burlesque melodrama – understood as the direct critical parody of the mode – accompanied melodrama throughout its rise and its decline, and it remains a moot point whether parody contributed to either. But theatrical parody in the period extended to all forms of theatre. There were innumerable parodies of Shakespeare in the course of the century, and of opera also: Gilbert and Sullivan emerge from this tradition of operatic burlesque, and parody remained a central aspect of their comic operas throughout. These forms were accompanied by extravaganzas which parodied fairy tales and classical mythology. In the words of Michael Booth, the foremost historian of nineteenth-century theatre, 'from at least Isaac Pocock's *The Maid and the Magpie* (1815) ... almost every really successful melodrama, opera and "drama" was spiritedly and usually promptly burlesqued' (Booth, 1976: 34).

It is nevertheless possible to trace, within this deeply carnivalised situation, a tradition of burlesque melodrama, beginning with *The Earls of Hammersmith*, and continuing through such famous (or notorious) parodies as *The Miller and his Men, A Burlesque*

Mealy-Drama (1860) by Francis Talfourd and Henry J. Byron, to many further parodies of melodrama at the end of the century and beyond. Though Booth argues that the authors of burlesque had no clear satirical target, the plots and conventions of melodrama were certainly the objects of parody, and more generally the burlesques sought to subject the elevation of melodrama to comic reduction. A stage direction in Talfourd and Byron's *The Miller and his Men* describes a character as 'Descending to Commonplace', a description that encapsulates the basic premise of burlesque, which, by juxtaposing the elevated and the commonplace, seeks to expose the former. But it is certainly possible to recognise, as most critics of burlesque melodrama have done, that such assaults on melodrama could be 'affectionate', and indeed could be written by authors who themselves wrote 'straight' examples of the mode.

Here, certainly, is an example of an 'affectionate' parody, taken from *The Earls of Hammersmith*; this is a general parody, and the following scene mocks the conventions of the recognition scene (it should perhaps also be explained that Sir Walter is nine years old and in love with his grandmother):

LADY SIMPLE:	(*aside*)	Is it possible?
SIR WALTER:	(*aside*)	What's this?
LADY SIMPLE:	(*aside*)	Can it be? Yes; no!
SIR WALTER:	(*aside*)	No; yes.
LADY SIMPLE:	(*aside*)	Is it my son I see, or is it another?
SIR WALTER:	(*aside*)	Oh, yes!
LADY SIMPLE:		Oh, no!
SIR WALTER:	(*aside*)	It is, it is, my mother.
	(*embracing – bawls in her ear*)	Be secret, we're observed.
LADY SIMPLE:	(*bawling*)	I will.

(Lawler, 1811: 6)

This undoubtedly demonstrates some delighted scepticism with respect to the conventions of melodrama, and indeed towards the improbabilities of plotting that the mode habitually displayed. But this scepticism is not normative; that is, it does not presume some standard of drama where the probabilities are not flouted. On the contrary, in a similar manner to the eighteenth-century burlesques that preceded it, this play enjoys the absurdities and makes them an opportunity for some fantastic humour of its own – as in the delightful moment when the Ghost of a Footman in livery rises, and presents a note to Sir Walter, who reads as follows: 'The ghost of the dowager Countess of Hammersmith rises, and presents her compliments to Sir Walter Wisehead' (Lawler, 1811: 8). The coexistence of parody of this kind, with the mode that it parodies, is not difficult to explain.

Similarly, Talfourd and Byron's *The Miller and his Men, A Burlesque Mealy-Drama* (1860), which parodies Isaac Pocock's much-performed *The Miller and his Men* of 1813, takes pleasure in playing with the conventions of the melodramatic mode, as in the following scene when the heroine of the play is very pleased that her father is angry with her, and then disappointed that he does not behave in a sufficiently tyrannical way:

CLAUDINE:	Severe? delicious! Angry? ecstasy!
	'Tis the first time you ever threatened me!
KELMAR:	My child!
CLAUDINE:	Oh dear! I beg you won't come round.
	If you would only dash me to the ground –
	Shut me up in my room – starve or ill-treat me –
KELMAR:	Don't be absurd.
CLAUDINE:	If you would only beat me,
	I should be *so* obliged.
KELMAR:	Nonsense! have done!
CLAUDINE: (*pettishly*)	Won't even let me be an 'injured one'.

(Talfourd and Byron, 1860: 8)

And this play demonstrates remorselessly one of the most prominent and insistent features of nineteenth-century burlesque: never-ending puns introduced at any and every opportunity:

COUNT: Oh, dear, oh dear, I am – *oh dear*, afraid,
           There's more *owed here* than ever can be paid.

                                        (ibid.: 15)

However, despite its evident pleasure in the absurdities of melodrama, this is more like a conflictual parody than *The Earls of Hammersmith*, or indeed than the many extravaganzas and burlesques which were contemporary to it. The part that parody may have played in the decline of melodrama will be discussed shortly.

Alongside these parodies of melodrama, there existed the related forms of the extravaganza, and, in the later nineteenth century, the burlesque, when the form finally dared to speak its name. The acknowledged master of the extravaganza was J.R. Planché (1796–1880), who defined it in these terms: 'distinguishing the whimsical treatment of a poetical subject from the broad caricature of a tragedy, which was correctly described as a burlesque' (quoted in Booth, 1976: 11). Planché's 'fairy' and 'classical' extravaganzas, such as *Fortunio and his Seven Gifted Servants* and *The Golden Fleece; or Jason's Colchas, and Medea in Corinth*, from the 1840s and 1850s, combine the whimsy that he describes, with recollections of Shakespeare, mild burlesque of melodrama, and musical jokes; the latter play, in so far as it treats the story of Jason and Medea, depends upon an almost traditional interchange between grand topic and low slang, perhaps making it closer to the seventeenth century tradition of classical *travesty* than burlesque theatre. In the 1860s, extravaganza developed into the entertainment known as the burlesque. An example is F.C. Burnand's *Paris, or Vive Lemprière* (1866), in which Jupiter, Mercury and Apollo were all played by women, while the shepherdess Oenone was played by a man; in which there were references to

Offenbach, contemporary products, and topical jokes; in which there was a balloon-descent, pugilism and conjuring tricks; which ended with a grand attitude; and in which the standard of the non-stop punning is indicated by the title (Lemprière was the standard reference book on classical mythology; 'Vive l'Empereur' was the 'God Save the King' of the France of the Second Empire). In a way similar to Planché's classical extravaganzas, the dialogue, such as it is, depends upon the usual exchanges between the high and the low. Theatre of this kind bespeaks a cultural situation which is so thoroughly secularised that the once-prestigious forms have become little more than an opportunity for fancy cross-dressing. Out of entertainments of this kind, properly called 'burlesque', the American theatre developed the kind of entertainment known under that title and still current today.

Finally, in this brief account of the parodic forms of the nineteenth-century theatre, mention should be made of the innumerable travesties of Shakespeare that were written and performed in the period. These ranged from the more learned parody, such as John Poole's *Hamlet Travestie* (1812) – whose satirical target is really learned commentators rather than Shakespeare himself – to shorter plays and sketches, such as Maurice Dowling's *Othello Travestie, an Operatic Burlesque Burletta* (1834) or Francis Talfourd's *Macbeth, somewhat removed from the text of Shakespeare* (1848). These were the small change of the nineteenth-century theatre, travestying the plays of Shakespeare into comic rhyming couplets, and including musical parodies of well-known tunes:

DESDEMONA:	*(to the tune of 'Bonnie Laddie')*	
	Once while darning father's stocking,	Too Ral, &c.
	Oh! he told a tale so shocking;	Too Ral, &c.
	So romantic – yet so tender,	
	That I fell fainting 'cross the fender.	Too Ral, &c.

Once again, although the basic joke here depends upon the comic

interchange between high and low, this is a travesty that scarcely
touches the position of the original.

However, there was an anxiety in the nineteenth century that
burlesque would indeed damage the authors and the modes that
it took such pleasure in mocking – 'affectionately' or otherwise –
and with a consideration of this possibility we can conclude this
chapter. Certainly John Poole, the author of *Hamlet Travestie* in
1812, prefaced his parody with an extensive apologia, defending
it against the charge that parody might be damaging: 'The objection commonly urged against burlesques and parodies in general,
is, that they tend to bring into ridicule and contempt those
authors against whose works they are directed' (1812: 3). Poole
considered Shakespeare safe against such ridicule, but considered
his commentators to be fair game, hence his extensive parody of
footnotes and the other paraphernalia of scholarly editions. But
he voices as an anxiety, what later critics of the nineteenth-century theatre would announce as a fact, that burlesque did help to
kill off the modes that it mocked. Effectively, it was claimed (as it
was at intervals in the eighteenth century) that burlesque *worked*,
in that it brought into permanent disrepute the elevated modes
that it parodied. Thus the theatre critic Clement Scott wrote in
1880 that 'the old days of mouthing and ranting – penny plain
and twopence coloured – are over, burlesque has killed them, and
if they were to arise they would be hooted down' (quoted in
Booth, 1976: 34). Michael Booth argues the case more fully:

> Essentially good-natured and affectionate towards its originals though
> burlesque melodrama was, nevertheless it was eventually destructive.
> By the beginning of the twentieth century a substantial and influential
> portion of the middle-class audience could no longer take the tradi-
> tional conventions and situations of melodrama seriously. The cumu-
> lative effect of so much burlesque, so much genial contempt for the
> sacred articles of melodramatic faith, must have been a factor in the
> decline of melodrama. Such burlesque reflected the advanced views

of the iconoclast and educated audiences in the process of disbelief.

(Booth, 1976: 34)

While there is something inevitably speculative about this position ('*must have been* a factor'), it is nevertheless one that requires careful consideration.

A similar question was raised with respect to the burlesquing of heroic drama in the eighteenth century: did that contribute to the decline of the genre? These questions are extraordinarily difficult to answer. We need to consider simple matters of chronology; for example, both heroic tragedy and melodrama were accompanied by burlesque from their very beginnings, which would suggest that the elevated modes and their accompanying parodies could coexist without difficulty over long stretches of time. In this case, we would need to find some other explanation, more social or historical, for the decline of these modes. The lengthy coexistence of high modes and their parodic counterparts also challenges simplified Bakhtinian notions of novelisation as a once and for all event. At the very least we would have to think of it as a process which extended over a period of more than two centuries, with local and temporary victories for the desacralising genres, and continual reinvention of the elevated ones. Indeed, there is a case for considering melodrama as a kind of populist version of heroic tragedy, carrying into the nineteenth century, in more petty-bourgeois accents, the heroic elevation that could not be sustained in the more archaic genre. It would be better to think of the life and death of genres as epochal events, reflecting profound alterations in the social history and composition of the societies in which the genres live and to which they speak. The importance of parody, and the credence given to it, would in this view be a symptom of those alterations; the contribution of burlesque to the demise of heroic tragedy or melodrama would be real, but it would itself be enabled by other and more fundamental social or historical changes.

The decline of melodrama in the theatre at the end of the nineteenth century must clearly be placed alongside its decline in other forms as well: in the novel, for example, or in painting. It is hard not to see this as part of a wider cultural and social shift in which substantial sections of the educated classes repudiated many of the dominant cultural forms of the nineteenth century under the impact of modernity. However, it is also the case that while melodrama may have disappeared from the canons of high culture, including the elite theatre, it was to have a vigorous afterlife in the popular culture of the twentieth century, in film and television as much as in books and magazines. And in this diverse and proliferating popular culture, parody also plays a prominent role.

Parody in the twentieth-century theatre, however, was much more sporadic than in its nineteenth-century predecessor. Some of the conventions of burlesque theatre were continued in music hall and other popular theatrical forms, to be partly assimilated by popular cinema or finally to be replaced by it. In the absence of any single dominant tradition of high theatrical seriousness, there was no accompanying tradition of its burlesque. Individual playwrights used parodic or second-order forms extensively, most notably Tom Stoppard in the British theatre, whose *Rosencrantz and Guildenstern are Dead* (1967), *The Real Inspector Hound* (1968), and *Travesties* (1974) all make sophisticated use of parody. In another direction, there was an intermittent theatrical form in which some of the cinematic conventions of Hollywood were parodied, such as *The Rocky Horror Show* (1973) or *Return to the Forbidden Planet* (1988); these parodied respectively the conventions of the horror film and the science fiction movie, and in their playfulness, punning, musical jokes and self-conscious deflations resembled nothing so much as the theatrical burlesques of the 1860s. But these were occasional features of twentieth-century theatre; overall, it is hard to avoid the conclusion that the decline of theatre as a popular art form was sufficient to entail the decline of theatrical burlesque also.

6

IS NOTHING SACRED?

Parody and the postmodern

In an influential essay, 'The Politics of Self-Parody', published in *The Partisan Review* in 1968, Richard Poirier linked discussions of parody with developments in writing that have come to be known as postmodernism. Poirier set himself the task of describing a kind of newly developed writing, 'a literature of self-parody that makes fun of itself *as it goes along*' (Poirier, 1968: 339). Taking Joyce and Nabokov as his exemplary writers, Poirier distinguished between a traditional practice of parody which retained some sense of the controlling force of 'life or history', and those writers who were conscious of the provisional nature of all discursive constructions. While Poirier's essay certainly did not initiate the connection between parody and postmodernism (a connection made more insistently in the discussion of architecture) it is symptomatic of a widespread position which equates postmodernist cultural forms with formal self-consciousness, epistemological relativism (the belief that there can be no secure ground to belief), and parody. Poirier's article was a modest if important attempt to characterise one trend in contemporary writing. In the 1980s and 1990s, however, there developed a proliferating set of arguments under the heading of 'postmodernism', which concern not only art and architecture but also the nature of late capitalism and contemporary society. Extraordinary as it may seem, the nature of parody has been a significant strand in these debates.

The most significant moment in this extension in the range of argument was a famous essay in the *New Left Review* in 1984, in which Fredric Jameson succeeded in giving debates about parody a prominence that they had never previously enjoyed (Jameson, 1984). The key move that Jameson made was to link the argument about parody and postmodernism to a description of late capitalism; in brief, postmodernist art forms were peculiarly expressive of the logic of the contemporary economy. Jameson's argument was briefly this: that the cultural logic of late capitalism was distinct from that of previous economic stages; that postmodernist cultural practice in a range of arts expressed this cultural logic; that this cultural practice was characterised above all by pastiche, which was to be distinguished from parody by the absence of any critical distance from the ur-text. Jameson's essay characterised 'consumer' or 'late capitalist' or 'post-industrial' society as a world without cultural hierarchies; a depthless world in which the recourse to nature, or the past, or 'high' culture, as ways of getting the measure of the world, has been abandoned. In such a situation, the critical force carried by parody (and evident in the parodic practices of modernism, for example in *The Waste Land*) has been replaced by pastiche, in which artists, architects and writers can endlessly allude to other styles in an interminable recycling which mirrors the unending commodity circulation of an absolutely extensive capitalism.

Whatever credence is to be afforded to Jameson's argument in this essay, it does represent the germinal moment in current discussions of postmodernism and parody, and in this final chapter I shall use it, and responses to it, as a way of charting these contemporary debates. As Jameson himself notes in another essay written at about the same time, arguments about postmodernism readily resolve themselves into profound political disagreements about the cultural direction of the contemporary world (Jameson,

1988). Taking my cue from his effort to map these positions, I will similarly map various responses to Jameson's essay, as they press upon the cultural logic, not of capitalism, but, more modestly, of parody. I shall begin by addressing that fundamental distinction between parody and pastiche.

An initial response to this aspect of Jameson's essay is simply to assert that the distinction between parody and pastiche is mistaken or unsustainable. This is the view taken by Linda Hutcheon in *A Poetics of Postmodernism* (1988), where she contends that Jameson has been misled by the notion of parody as ridiculing imitation; if, on the contrary, it is recognised that parody need not have that ridiculing or critical edge, then Jameson's distinction falls, and with it one of the central contentions of his argument. There is an evident force to this objection; on the other hand, it is argument by definition, which affects the terms in which the discussion about postmodernism should be conducted, but not the substance. Conceding that parody can act more like pastiche as Jameson defines it, in a non-critical or 'depthless' way, does not in the least affect his assertion that culture of this (parodic or pastiche-like) kind can be considered the cultural dominant of late capitalism. However, it does mean that we can conduct the debate about parody in postmodernism using the term itself, recognising that some latitude of definition can conceal important questions of cultural politics. And we will recall that the parodic forms do not lend themselves to hard-and-fast distinctions, but are better understood as a continuum or spectrum of formal possibilities.

The first position that logically presents itself is that of Linda Hutcheon herself, who, despite the caveat that she makes with respect to the distinction between parody and pastiche, argues that parody in postmodern architecture (the terrain on which she chooses to contest Jameson) is characterised by precisely that critical edge that Jameson had sought to void it of. Drawing heavily on the work of Charles Jencks, she argues that the multiple allusions to the past, made by architecture of this kind, have exactly the function of mobilising in the present the historic weight or speci-ficity of the quoted styles, putting them at an ironic or critical distance from the contemporary spaces into which they are inserted. This is a sophisticated defence of parody in architecture, seeing its practice as inserting into the contemporary moment buildings which self-consciously allude to the historical past, with varying degrees of irony about the impossibility of repeating that past. Hutcheon's position, then, is one which celebrates post-modern parody, in architecture at least; here the allusive practices of postmodernism mark a decisive step forward from what, in this context, are seen as the aridity and prescriptivism of Modernism. Parody is the mark of a gameful but productive relationship with the past which nevertheless demonstrates the persistence of criti-cal distance into the high art of the present.

A very different objection to Jameson, and one that is logically and politically opposite, comes from John Docker in *Postmodernism and Popular Culture* (1994). Drawing on Bakhtin's notion of carni-val, Docker argues for the pervasiveness of parody in contempo-rary mass-cultural forms, seeing these latter as acting in closely comparable ways to the carnival forms of the Renaissance. Thus soap opera, an exemplary mass-cultural form, is a heterogeneous mode, which includes both seriousness (melodrama) and parody. Indeed, melodrama itself becomes formally inclusive, in the man-ner of Bakhtin's 'novel', in this account. Effectively, Docker asserts the persistence of parody in popular-cultural forms, cer-tainly from the nineteenth century onwards; his argument is that there is nothing specifically 'postmodern' about parody, rather that 'postmodernism' permits us to appreciate the role of parody in popular culture in a way that the high-cultural commitments of modernism did not.

Like Hutcheon, Docker argues partly by definition; in his gen-eral hostility to Jameson he contends that the latter's argument is false because the building which he discusses is really a modernist and not a postmodernist one. Once again we can see that this is a distinction which does little to affect the substance of Jameson's argument. Far more important is the general case that Docker makes with respect to popular culture and the place of parody within it. Popular culture persists in the variety and gusto which have always characterised it, in its relish for carnivalesque forms, including parody; 'postmodernism' is a name for that break with modernism which allows us to speak positively of popular culture. Thus Docker contends that parody does indeed characterise postmodern culture, but that its source is in popular culture, now validated by the collapse of the elite commitments of modernism. Seeing Jameson as yet another proponent of those anti-popular prejudices, Docker seeks to contradict him at every point. Postmodern artistic practice is characterised by parody and not pastiche; its provenance is the rich history of popular-cultural forms, understood in Bakhtinian terms; and a positive assessment of postmodern culture is to be based on these commitments and not the (differing) high art ones of both Jameson and Hutcheon.

Judging from these objections, it would seem that Jameson's essay is to be read as a lament for the high seriousness and high culture of modernism, from which the parodic forms of postmodernism, emptied of critical edge, are a disastrous falling-off. This indeed is one logical position, and it could be hostile to all forms of parody, or merely to the non-critical kind described by Jameson as pastiche. However, it is not the position which Jameson himself adopts, which is more properly described as a *dialectical* one; or at least, it aspires to be so characterised. A properly Marxist cultural politics could never simply lament the cultural forms of the past, and wish to reinvent them as though they could be produced by an act of will and against the current of history. Rather, in the manner of Brecht's injunction to start from the bad new things rather than the good old ones, Jameson's essay is at once an anatomy of the cultural logic of late capitalism and an exploration of its positive cultural possibilities.

Nevertheless, it is certainly possible to find or to imagine a cultural politics hostile to postmodernist parody in both the high art form defended by Hutcheon and the popular-cultural practices upheld by Docker. Hostility to 'modern art', parodic or otherwise, has been one of the characteristic notes of journalism for the last half century at least. And the occasional lament about the triviality and parasitism of contemporary culture, while increasingly infrequent, can still be heard as one response to the dominance of popular over high culture in the postmodern world. Hostility to the pervasiveness of parody in the postmodern world (in the related form of travesty) can also emerge from the perception that its proliferation is caused by media capitalism (see Karrer, 1997). Given this variety of possible positions with respect to postmodernism and the place of parody within it, it would be helpful to make some elementary and preliminary distinctions.

Let us begin by asking whether there is indeed something distinctive about the contemporary cultural moment which has given a special prominence to parody and its related forms. One of the strengths of Jameson's essay is that it seeks to bring into view what he describes as a cultural dominant, by which he means not that the postmodernist art forms that he describes are in any sense statistically dominant in cultural production, but that they express with a particular aptness the social-cultural characteristics of our period. The notion of a cultural dominant could even be thought of as an analytical device, designed to make visible the particular contours of the world that surrounds us. In the course of the essay, Jameson entertains the possibility that the notion is nevertheless unsustainable: 'If we do not achieve some general sense of a cultural dominant, then we fall back into a view of present history as sheer heterogeneity, random difference, a coexistence of a host of distinct forces whose effectivity is undecidable' (Jameson, 1984: 57). It may be that it is just this possibility that we have to confront in asking whether anything distinguishes the contemporary world with respect to its parodic practice, both at the level of high art or, following Docker, in the massively diffused products of popular culture.

To begin with the question at the level of high culture: that is, of literary novels, poetry, gallery art, architecture, theatre, and art films. We need to ask whether parodic forms make up the cultural dominant of the contemporary moment in a way that is significantly different from that of previous periods. This is not just a question of listing the cultural products of the moment which include parody: the novels of Alasdair Gray, John Barth, Salman Rushdie and Jonathan Coe, the architecture of Portoghesi or Philip Johnson, the poetry of Tony Harrison, the art of Andy Warhol or Gilbert and George. It is rather that we have to decide whether such art is in an authentic way a contemporary cultural dominant, when it would be perfectly possible both to construct a list of contemporary writers, artists and architects whose work was in no sense parodic, and to find moments in the past when parody has been just as central a feature of cultural production. I have considered two such moments in the course of this book: the Early Modern period of Cervantes and Jacobean drama, and the moment of mock-heroic a century later. In the light of these considerations, it seems impossible to me to assert that there is anything distinctive or central about parody, at the level of high art, which differentiates the postmodern world from its predecessors. This is not to deny the importance of parody in contemporary art and literature, which I shall discuss shortly. But it is to deny that this form leads towards any particular insight into the cultural dominant of the contemporary world.

This may seem a perversely literal-minded way of pursuing this question, especially when it is considered that postmodernism is supposed to break down the distinctions between high and popular culture. And there is clearly no denying the prevalence of parody and its related forms in the productions of popular culture. Let us consider them for a moment, as we settle down to an evening's entertainment on the box. We begin with *The*

Simpsons, broadly parodic of the suburban family of the sit-coms and the soaps, and full of specific parodies of Hollywood films, as well as including a parody of another cartoon, *Tom and Jerry*. We can move on from there to any number of soap operas, which, as Docker has pointed out, move in and out of melodrama and parody as the demands of the story line and the ratings dictate. We can then zap between two self-confessed comedy shows, one of which has as its staple the parody of pop videos, films, and other television drama, while the other is the vehicle for an impersonator. This one (Rory Bremner) has genuine and legitimate satiric intentions; over on one of the satellite channels, however, they are running repeats of another impersonator (Mike Yarwood) whose political intentions were precisely non-existent. After these comic slots, one of the main broadcast networks is showing a talent show which requires contestants to imitate famous pop or country singers; they do so with varying degrees of parodic exactness. Then there is a choice between two comedy quiz-shows, one about pop music and the other about sport; both involve local and generally embarrassing parodies of one group of 'celebrities' by another. In between these programmes we can linger on the adverts, full of parodic allusions to popular music, films, and other television programmes. Finally we can channel-hop between two films, one a parody disaster-movie, the other a remake, with an undecidable ironic charge, of a classic Hollywood film of the 1940s.

What this evening's entertainment suggests is a raucous and multivocal culture, in which the traditional cultural hierarchies have broken down. In general, Docker's account of this situation is surely persuasive; what has happened here is that the long-standing parodic energies of popular culture have been unleashed or validated. To call this 'postmodern' is no more than to say that modernist disdain for the popular no longer has the authority that it once had. There has therefore been a profound cultural and social shift in societies massively penetrated by the mass media, and this transformation requires careful analysis. However, this shift does not justify the notion of parody playing a significant part in any contemporary cultural dominant. What it rather suggests is indeed, in Jameson's words, a 'coexistence of a host of distinct forces whose effectivity is undecidable'; within each of those distinct forces parody and its related practices have varying degrees of prominence and are more or less playful, critical, ironic, or empty.

This general situation does nevertheless call out for some more general explanation of a properly social-historical kind. If we are to see it as the final unleashing of popular-cultural energies which extend over several centuries, then perhaps an epochal explanation of a Bakhtinian kind is appropriate. In such an account, the current predominance of popular-cultural forms of a parodic kind could be seen as the culmination of an epochal process of novelisation, in which the multiple sources of cultural authority in society have been progressively exposed to relativising or parodic underminings. What began with Rabelais ends with *The Simpsons*. The trouble with such a grand narrative, however, is that it is *too* epochal, insufficiently alert to the more 'micro' and properly historical forces acting in society at any period. What is rather needed is a description of the multiple and varying sources of cultural authority in society, and the capacity of any social order to invent and to reinvent its sacred words as beliefs change, different social classes take the social lead, differing cultural forms come into and move out of prominence.

Thus we would need to trace the continuities between nineteenth-century popular-cultural forms and the predominant late twentieth-century ones. There are indeed some striking continuities; melodrama, for example, may or may not have been laughed off the London West End stage, but its persistence into silent cinema, Hollywood, and soap opera is clearly visible. The elaborate theatrical entertainments of the 1860s may not have survived, but many of the local forms pioneered there persisted in variety and the music hall, and eventually made their way into 'Light

Entertainment' on the television – and the genie is now, not out of the box, but everywhere on it. Even the panel games and chat shows which seem so essentially televisual can trace their ancestry in part to the decorous entertainments of the Victorian parlour. None of which is to say that they could have the same meanings in their transformed new surroundings; quite the contrary, indeed. Clearly these meanings, and the uses to which these forms can be put, are transformed as these forms take on their contemporary predominance. But this is not to say that nothing is now sacred. It may now be permissible to parody religion or the Royal Family, but there are severe limits placed around the spaces available for such parodies (as Salman Rushdie can testify after the publication of *Satanic Verses*), and new sacred topics can appear which are put beyond the bounds of acceptable humour. Such limits may be right and appropriate; readers can decide for themselves on the value of a parody of the Holocaust movie *Schindler's List*, or Elton John's tribute record to Princess Diana, 'Candle in the Wind'. Rather than think of 'novelisation' as one epochal process, it is better to conceive of each historical moment as characterised by its own balance of authoritative and parodic forms, and as generating its own sacred texts. It is certainly the case that in some periods the parodic forms are more pervasive, more audible, more raucous even, than in others. But this is not a permanent transformation; *mutatis mutandis*, and the decorousness of the 1950s may well return.

In the remainder of this chapter, I will consider some of the contemporary cultural forms in which parody plays an important role. There is no effort here to trace a cultural dominant, but there will be an attempt to locate these cultural forms within the social conflicts and culture wars of the present moment. What I am suggesting, in short, is a plural account of the place of parody in contemporary culture. It certainly serves particular cultural purposes, which vary from art form to art form, and within the various genres of popular culture. However, I do not believe that the apparent convergence between 'high' and 'popular' forms is indicative of a general cultural dominant; rather, parody serves differing (and significant) purposes within the widely various cultural domains that constitute the contemporary world.

PARODY IN THE POSTMODERNIST NOVEL

Let us begin by tracing the place of parody in high-art literary forms, especially in the novel, where a recognisable local form of formally self-conscious and highly allusive novel is described as 'postmodernist'. A range of novelists within the last thirty years have written novels which include more or less of parody and pastiche, in ways which push them towards formal self-consciousness, and which involve recycling and reassessing the cultural forms of the past. Consider the following list (doubtless other readers could construct lists with different national emphases): John Barth, *The Sot-Weed Factor* (1965), Jonathan Bate, *The Cure for Love* (1998), Malcolm Bradbury, *Who Do You Think You Are?* (1976), Antonia Byatt, *Possession* (1990), Peter Carey, *Oscar and Lucinda* (1988) and *Jack Maggs* (1998), Jonathan Coe, *What a Carve Up!* (1994), Umberto Eco, *The Name of the Rose* (1980) and *Foucault's Pendulum* (1989), John Fowles, *The French Lieutenant's Woman* (1969), Alasdair Gray, *Lanark* (1981), and David Lodge, *The British Museum is Falling Down* (1965) and *Small World* (1984). While all these novels vary widely, they nevertheless share the common characteristic of reusing specific cultural productions from the past in ways which, at the very least, indicate both some connection to, and some distance from, their predecessors.

It is important nevertheless to make some distinctions. Most novelists, it can be said, engage in at least some linguistic imitation, by which they differentiate the voices of their characters, try to fill out the discursive world that they inhabit, or more generally indicate some of the linguistic 'static' which surrounds us all. This is part of the novelist's stock-in-trade. We have seen, in

Chapter 3, how this widespread characteristic of the form can be readily extended to become more or less systematic parody. While such imitation can certainly be found in these novels, what distinguishes them is the more explicit evocations of particular forms, or even particular works, which enable them to work in at least two cultural registers at once, engaged in the typically parodic procedure of 'double-coding', the term coined by Charles Jencks to describe the way that postmodern buildings make allusion at once to an anterior style and to the moment of construction. Thus Jonathan Bate's novel *The Cure for Love* evokes William Hazlitt's *Liber Amoris* (1823), as well as other writing by the great essayist, to tell a story of sexual infatuation; the novel moves in and out of direct quotation and pastiche to create a complex series of resonances between the language of the early nineteenth century and the present moment. Antonia Byatt's novel *Possession*, self-consciously styled 'a romance', goes to extraordinary lengths to create a series of mock nineteenth-century poems, letters and fairy stories, as well as more recognisably parodic recreations of contemporary literary criticism, to establish multiple interactions between the cultural concerns of the late twentieth century and those of a century earlier. Comparable invocations and parodic inventions mark all the novels that I have listed and indicate something of the sense of cultural belatedness which, understood in both positive and negative ways, characterises this kind of writing.

A further distinction needs to be made between the varying degrees of seriousness with which these novelists deploy parody, which is not the same thing as their differing comic power, since writing can be both comic and serious at the same time. Perhaps it would be better to say that some of these novelists use parody as a form of display; or, to put the case less aggressively, writing such as David Lodge's *The British Museum is Falling Down*, or still more the collection of parodies in Malcolm Bradbury's *Who Do You Think You Are?*, is best understood as descending from the model of literary parody exemplified in Max Beerbohm's *A Christmas Garland*. Such parody is done for the fun of it; little structural point emerges from it in novelistic terms, though it may of course be literary criticism conducted by other means. And in this context, it is worth noting the high percentage of these novelists who have strong connections with the academy or are actually practising academic literary critics: five out of the ten names on my list. While this certainly says something about the provenance and readership of the contemporary literary novel, it is perhaps also indicative of the culturally and socially specific location which we ought to recognise as the home of this kind of 'postmodernist' novel.

I propose to consider two of these novels more closely, in order to get a better idea of the role of parody in them, and to explore both the process of double-coding which characterises them at their most interesting, and that sense of cultural belatedness to which perhaps they testify. Antonia Byatt's *Possession* is the novel which goes to greatest length to create a parodic world, in which she recreates a variety of competing (or complementary) discourses from both the nineteenth and twentieth centuries. In an act of almost perverse inventiveness, she creates two new major nineteenth-century poets, one of whom is not dissimilar from Robert Browning, while the other resembles, to some extent at least, Christina Rossetti. The novel contains substantial 'quotations' from both their works – which are in fact elaborate parodies of the work of nineteenth-century writers like the two mentioned, but of other writers also. It is not a coincidence, perhaps, that the family name of the wife of the Browning-like poet should be Calverley, a reference to the most celebrated of Browning's parodists, C.S. Calverley. The plot of the whole novel turns on the discovery of a cache of letters exchanged between the two poets, which are reproduced in a pastiche of nineteenth-century epistolary style. Additionally, since the novel is mostly set in the contemporary literary academy, there is plentiful opportunity for parody of the competing discourses which jostle with each other in that world, including the staid literary-biographical, the psychoanalytic, and the deconstructive.

Familiar difficulties of definition present themselves immediately, however, in any attempt to describe *Possession*, since it is unclear whether the poems of the invented poet Randolph Ash, or those of the 'Fairy poet' Christabel LaMotte, should be described as parody or pastiche. They certainly are not hostile parodies in the manner of Calverley's 'The Cock and the Bull' (see p. 116-17). Consider the following poem, one of many Browning-like poems included in the novel:

> Since riddles are the order of the day
> Come here, my love, and I will tell thee one.
>
> There is a place to which all Poets come
> Some having sought it long, some unawares,
> Some having battled monsters, some asleep
> Who chance upon the past in thickest dream,
> Some lost in mythy mazes, some direct
> From fear of death, or lust of life or thought
> And some who lost themselves in Arcady ...
>
> These things are there. The garden and the tree
> The serpent at its root, the fruit of gold
> The woman in the shadow of the boughs
> The running water and the grassy space.
>
> (Byatt, 1991: 463)

This clearly is not hostile parody; Byatt has invented her own nineteenth-century poetic idiom, which has to be accepted as genuinely good poetry if the basic premise of the novel is to be accepted. This is so much the case that a reading of this particular poem has the force of an illumination for the novel's hero, who is provoked by it into a recognition of his own poetic vocation. It is nearer to pastiche, though in this instance Byatt has moved away from the more direct pastiche of Browning that characterises some of her other invented poems.

By contrast, there are elements of more directly parodic writing in the novel, as in this extract from the standard scholarly biography of Roland Ash, called *The Great Ventriloquist*:

> So on a clear June day in 1848 the poet and his new bride made their way along the shady river bank to the cavern which shelters the sources of the Sorgue, a sight awesome and sublime enough to satisfy even the most romantic traveller and how much more impressive when conjoined with the memory of the great courtly lover, Petrarch, living out there the days of his devotion and the horror of learning of his mistress's death of the plague.

(ibid.: 108)

The extract continues in a similar vein of mock-scholarly biography for several pages. This certainly has more of a critical edge than the pastiche-poem by Ash; Byatt is parodying a certain pomposity in the style here, coupled with the display of exhaustive scholarship. But even here she is prepared to allow a certain validity to this mode of discourse, which is one among the many which jostle with each other in the book. In each case, the reader is required to consider the degree of critical distance with which the prose is offered; such negotiations cannot be captured by hard-and-fast distinctions between parody and pastiche.

However, while it is certainly the case that the novel is made up largely of this writing in the parodic mode, there is also a narrative conducted in a contemporary idiom. The very point of the novel, indeed, is to contrast the characteristic habits of mind and behaviour of the nineteenth century with that of the late twentieth. This works at the level of parody; the pastiche of nineteenth-century writing is partly understood through the parody of twentieth-century literary criticism. But the structure of the book allows a series of contrasts and comparisons to be developed, by which the reader is enabled to read contemporary behaviour in the light of the nineteenth century. This is exactly a form of 'double-coding'; while on the one hand the secret about Roland Ash and Christabel LaMotte to which the narrative moves is a sexual one, conversely the novel seeks to expose the inadequacy of exclusively sexual twentieth-century explanations of human behaviour. The parodies and pastiches of the novel cut both ways, enabling the reader to assess the behaviour of both centuries in the discursive frames of each other.

Byatt discusses this proliferation of connections explicitly, in a moment of narratorial reflection itself reminiscent of the nineteenth-century novel:

> Roland thought, partly with precise postmodernist pleasure, and partly with a real element of superstitious dread, that he and Maud were being driven by a plot or fate that seemed, at least possibly, to be not their plot or fate but that of those others. And it is probable that there is an element of superstitious dread in any self-referring, self-reflexive, inturned postmodernist mirror-game or plot-coil that recognises that it has got out of hand, that connections proliferate apparently at random, that is to say, with equal verisimilitude, apparently in response to some ferocious ordering principle, not controlled by conscious intention, which would of course, being a good postmodernist intention, *require* the aleatory or the multivalent or the 'free', but structuring, but controlling, but driving, to some – to what? – end.

> (Byatt, 1991: 421–2)

The novel moves toward its 'end', which is that of sexual consummation – 'possession' – in the contemporary plot, and of partial redemption in the fictional nineteenth-century world. In one sense this *is* explicable at the level of 'intention', however postmodernist or aleatory: the only fate driving these stories is that of their writer. But Byatt is nevertheless surely right to point to the proliferation of connections that the 'plot-coil' permits, which is partly created by her remarkable scholarly knowledge of the nineteenth century, but which is also facilitated or enabled by the pastiches and parodies which juxtapose the discursive styles of the two periods and in which these 'aleatory' connections proliferate.

Possession is not predominantly a comic novel, and, as that last quotation reveals, there is a confident narrative voice ordering the whole construction. Therefore, while the novel is certainly knowing about its own fictiveness, that knowledge is present as a frame which surrounds the novel, and is not used to investigate in any profound or undermining way the status of fiction or story-telling as such. The point of the novel, one might say, apart from the traditional novelistic pleasures of narrative excitement, subtleties of characterisation, and so on, is its juxtaposition of then and now. One important strand of contemporary culture, therefore, which we can call postmodernist in the restricted formal sense that Byatt herself uses, relies upon parody and its related modes to 'double-code' the present. The comparison may seem far-fetched, but we have noticed how, with comparable ironies and two-way traffic, the late seventeenth century and the early eighteenth century similarly used the cultural past to unlock the complexities of the present moment. For them, in Dryden's phrase, 'the second temple was not like the first'; the past, that is, provided artistic models which exceeded the achievements of the present. In the neoclassical world, the artistic past undoubtedly had a greater cultural authority than it does for us; but in a novel like *Possession* something like the cultural authority of the nineteenth-century past is invoked to get a critical distance on the present.

We can see parody put to very different purposes in another 'postmodernist' novel, Jonathan Coe's *What a Carve Up!*, from which I have already quoted in Chapter 3 (see pp. 72–4). There, however, Coe's book featured in a one-sided history of the novel as a modern example of a long tradition of novel-writing which parodied other debased genres to bolster its own claims to realism. Now we can draw attention to the more profoundly destabilising and metafictional role of parody in the novel: the whole book repeats the plot of the film *What a Carve Up!*, it ends and begins with the same sentence in a way which suggests the snake-like tongue-in-mouth circularity of fabulation, and it is uncertain whether there is any master discourse, or language of plain common sense, upon which readers can rely to order the multiple parodied jargons and dialects which constitute the novel. However, what distinguishes the novel quite markedly from *Possession* or the novels of Lodge or Bradbury is that it is driven by a political passion which makes it little less than a fierce and comic anatomy of contemporary Britain. In fact, the novel precisely fulfils the definition of postmodern parody as set out by Margaret Rose (1993); that is, it combines the metafictional and the comic. However, it does so in a way which is very much more serious than the fictions of the university writers which she brings forward as examples of what the genre should be.

Parody is certainly pervasive in the novel, which includes versions of a wide variety of recent and contemporary discourses: childish writing-exercises; company minutes; BBC interviews; erotic writing in novels; tabloid journalism; advertising and food-packaging; the political diary; magazine journalism of the *Tatler* and *Hello!* varieties. The novel is concerned with the massive social and political realignments of Britain in the 1980s, especially in the areas of popular journalism, the National Health Service, agriculture, and the 'defence industries' or arms trade; the parodies are addressed to the discursive transformations which accompanied these realignments. One telling pair of parodies, for example, contrasts two BBC interviews given by Henry Winshaw at different stages in his career; the first when he is a new Labour MP in 1960, the second when he is a Tory apologist for the NHS 'reforms' in the 1980s. In the first interview, an old-style BBC journalist is asking Winshaw about the coup in Iraq, in a series known as 'Backbencher':

BEAMISH: Finally, Mr Winshaw, do you see any irony in the fact that this coup – so hostile, potentially, to our national interests – has been carried out by an army trained and equipped by the British? Traditionally, the British and Iraqi governments have cooperated very closely in this area. Do you think their military ties will now be a thing of the past?

WINSHAW: Well, I very much hope not. I've always thought that the Iraqi military tie is an extremely attractive one, and I know there are many British officers who wear it with pride. So it would be a sad day for our country if that were to happen.

(Coe, 1995: 127)

This is a silly enough joke, but the whole interview does capture the atmosphere of high-minded public-service broadcasting, and technical incompetence, that characterised British television in the early 1960s. By contrast, when Winshaw is confronted by a critic of the NHS reforms on 1980's television, he responds in the following way:

17,000,000 over 5 years 12.3% of GDP 4% more than the EEC 35% up on the USSR 34,000 GPs for every HAS × 19.24 in real terms 9,586 for every FHSA seasonally adjusted 12,900,000 + 54.67 @ 19% incl VAT rising to 47% depending on IPR by the IHSM £4.52p NHS safe in our hands.

(Coe, 1995: 138)

This is a parody of the interview style of government ministers in the 1980s and 1990s who responded to all criticisms of government policy by a barrage of figures. But the more general point is the transition that has been made between differing televisual styles, the former patrician and polite, the latter populist and aggressive.

Perhaps the most tellingly parodic sections of the book, or at least, that area which gives Coe the greatest opportunity to exercise his parodic talents, are those which deal with tabloid journalism. Another Winshaw is a columnist on one of the popular papers; Coe supplies two examples of her journalistic style, printed in parallel columns:

A NEWSLETTER reaches my desk today from a group who call themselves the Supporters of Democracy in Iraq – or SODI for short.

They claim that President Saddam Hussein is a brutal dictator who maintains his power through torture and intimidation. Well, I've got some words of advice for this silly bunch of SODIs: *check your facts!*

It's not often that a television programme can make me feel physically sick, but last night was an exception.

Can there be anyone in the country whose stomach did not turn over as we watched Saddam Hussein on the *Nine O'Clock News*, parading the so-called 'hostages' he is wickedly proposing to use as a human shield?

The two columns continue to assert exactly opposite positions, in a brutally reductive parody of the debased idiom of tabloid editorialising. The comedy here is acrid and being put to sharp political effect.

Altogether *What a Carve Up!* offers a remarkable survey of, and assault upon, the myriad discourses that accompanied 'Thatcherism'. The whole novel is also built upon a structural parody of a 1950s' horror film of the same name. Indeed, the novel can only be described as 'postmodernist' because of these structurally parodic and self-reflexive features: self-reflexive because the structure of the book draws attention to the novel's own fictiveness, since its central character, in a book about the Winshaw family, is researching and writing a book about the Winshaw family. The novel concludes with a wonderfully ghoulish enactment of the gothic murders in the 1950s' horror film with which the story begins. However, while this playful and self-reflexive conclusion is part of the central premise of the novel, it has also to be said that it represents a kind of political hopelessness: the monstrous Winshaws, embodiment of a ruthless and aggressive ruling class, can only be killed off in playful fantasy. Thus, there is no master-narrative in the novel which can organise its material in the manner of the nineteenth-century realist novel, and in doing so point towards some politically and socially positive resolution of the ruling-class arrogance which it parodically assaults; the postmodernism of the novel is thus implicated in the wholesale defeat of the left in the last two decades of the twentieth century.

What a Carve Up!, then, has certain formal features which make it one of a group of contemporary postmodernist novels. However, some of its characteristics make it resemble Thackeray as much as Umberto Eco; which is not to say that Thackeray was a postmodernist novelist before the term was invented, but that 'postmodernism', understood as meaning a particular formal repertoire of parodic and metafictional devices, draws upon certain well-established capacities of the novel. For example, the prevalent use of parody in Coe's novel closely parallels Thackeray's practice in *Vanity Fair*, while the deliberately entertained fantasy conclusion is anticipated in *The Newcomes*. The important contrast is not between 'postmodernism' and 'realism', since *What a Carve Up!* quite loses its point if it is not understood as having some substantial purchase on the contemporary world. Rather, the formally distinguishing features of novels point to differing ways in which they are situated with respect to the actual transitions in the world to which they are addressed.

But if *What a Carve Up!* most closely resembles Thackeray, we need to re-examine that easy association of parody, even Richard Poirier's 'self-parody', with postmodernism. The transition that Poirier charts, between a realist parody which retains confidence in some modes of discourse, and a more fully sceptical parodic practice which is even sceptical of its own discursive constructions, is one that has been made at various points in the history of the novel, as I attempted to demonstrate in Chapter 3. The difficulty with that association, as in so many attempts at literary and cultural history, is the historical location of specific literary practices, by which the cultural characteristics of a period – 'modernist', or 'postmodernist' – are defined in formal terms. This kind of argument is always open to the counter-recognition that comparable forms can be found equally prominent at other moments of literary history. Thus it has become almost routine to cite *Tristram Shandy* as somehow anticipating postmodernism. This kind of confusion can be avoided only by recognising that contemporary postmodernist novels are activating formal possibilities that have long been present in the novel as a mode, though they do so in order to carry out particular cultural work in the present moment.

Other novels in this group situate themselves in differing ways, and each requires specific analysis. The general point to make with respect to parody, however, is that 'postmodernism' can best be understood in this context as a particular 'take' on the formal repertoire available to novelists; more precisely, as a move towards novelistic self-consciousness which drags into view other modes of discourse, other possible ways of understanding the world. Hence the greater or lesser inclusion of parody, imitation, pastiche or plagiarism in these novels. This opportunity presents itself in particular ways for those writers, especially from the former Empire, who wish to grasp the discourses that have been imposed upon them by imperialism and colonialism. It is to those writers, and the parodies which they use, to whom I now turn.

RECLAIMING THE METAPHOR

One of the central characters in Salman Rushdie's *Satanic Verses*, Saladin Chamcha, is an actor – 'an imitator of non-existing men', in his father's contemptuous words – who earns his money by his fantastic gift for mimicry. Indeed, he is one of the premier voice-over artists in the business: 'he made carpets speak in ware-house advertisements, he did celebrity impersonations, baked beans, frozen peas' (Rushdie, 1992: 60). Moreover, as a migrant to Britain, he has done everything in his power to take on the manners of the British: anglicising his name, changing his accent, adopting Anglo-centric views – his very name is a joke, for 'chamcha' in Hindi means spoon, and is the equivalent of 'toady' or 'arse-licker'. Rushdie is offering him as one possible mode of migrant 'assimila-tion', in which mimicry (or is it parody?) is central.

It is thus clear that the aesthetics of parody in this novel are caught up in the highly charged cultural negotiations involved in migration from former colonies to the metropolitan centre. They are also caught up in a more general account of personality, which, in an almost textbook Vološinovian manner (see p. 86), is described as made up of the fragments of imitated words taken in from the surrounding world, as in the following description of Saladin Chamcha's 'pathetic personality': 'that half-reconstructed affair of mimicry and voices' (Rushdie, 1992: 9). This is how Saladin is described elsewhere:

> A man who sets out to make himself up is taking on the Creator's role, according to one way of seeing things; he's unnatural, a blasphe-mer, an abomination of abominations. From another angle, you could see pathos in him, heroism in his struggle, in his willingness to risk: not all mutants survive. Or, consider him sociopolitically; most migrants learn, and can become disguises. Our own false descrip-tions to counter the falsehood invented about us, concealing for rea-sons of security our secret selves.
>
> A man who invents himself needs someone to believe in him, to prove he's managed it. Playing God again, you could say. Or you could come down a few notches, and think of Tinkerbell; fairies don't exist if children don't clap their hands. Or you might simply say: it's just like being a man.

(ibid.: 49)

So it is not sufficient to say that Saladin Chamcha's mimic personality is solely to be understood as a response to his migrant situation, though that *is* true; in a wider sense his situation is true of all of us.

The problem for Saladin in the novel, and indeed the problem for Salman Rushdie, is how to differentiate between authentic and inauthentic ways of being plural, multiple or self-constructed. Another way of saying this is to ask whether it is possible to differentiate between different politics of parody. If we are all made up of disguises, if our personalities are all a complicated mixture of mimicked or parodied voices, then there can be no notion of authenticity by which to measure the downright phoney. Yet the whole novel can be described as the political education of Saladin Chamcha, who has to learn to repudiate the elaborate parody of Englishness which he has assembled over the years in favour of some acknowledgement of his continuing Indianness.

The problem is further compounded by the fact that Indianness cannot be considered a simple or monologic or 'authentic' construction either. One of the many parodic inventions in the novel is a book by Saladin's Indian lover, which has the splendid title of *The Only Good Indian*. It is described as a book

on the confining myth of authenticity, that folkloristic straitjacket which she sought to replace by an ethic of historically validated eclecticism, for was not the entire national culture based on the principle of borrowing whatever clothes seemed to fit, Aryan, Mughal, British, take-the-best-and-leave-the-rest?

(ibid.: 52)

Both at the level of the individual personality, therefore, and at the level of national culture, there is no such thing as a single and undiluted whole; we are all shot through with mimicry, eclecticism, with a greater or lesser degree of parody. On what basis, therefore, can we distinguish between those who remain loyal to what they are from those opportunists who simply take on whatever colouring their environment suggests?

While this is certainly one of the questions raised by the novel, there is no doubt that in general it is aimed at promoting a cultural politics of pluralism and eclecticism. Indeed, the challenge that it poses to monotheistic Islam is made in comparable terms, persistently establishing oppositions between uncompromising adherence to an exclusive principle of oneness and the possibilities of compromise, proliferation, or contamination. In the politics of the contemporary world, the novel's commitment to the pluralistic side of that opposition does not lead to an unthinking liberalism but, among other things, to a very specific politics of parody, which can be pursued by following the writing of one of the minor characters in the book, Jumpy Joshi.

Jumpy is a poet and political activist, whose principal aesthetic strategy is to take the words of western culture and turn them against themselves. His most ambitious effort in this vein is an attempt to rewrite Enoch Powell's 'rivers of blood' speech – the 1968 outburst in which the prominent Conservative politician expressed, in racist language, his hostility to immigration by people of colour into Britain. In the following quotation Jumpy's poem *The River of Blood* is being maliciously described by someone who has discovered it in manuscript:

> 'he says the street is a river and we are the flow; humanity is the river of blood, that's the poet's point. Also the individual human being,' he broke off to run around to the far side of an eight-seater table as Jumpy came after him, blushing furiously, flapping his arms. 'In our very bodies, does the river of blood not flow?' *Like the Roman*, the ferrety Enoch Powell had said, *I seem to see the river Tiber foaming with much blood*. Reclaim the metaphor, Jumpy Joshi had told himself. Turn it; make it a thing we can use.

(ibid.: 186)

I read this as a politics of parody, specifically directed to the cultural situation of migrants who can 'turn' even the most abusive words of their oppressors, and redirect them for their own political purposes. Later in the book, another Joshi title appears – 'I Sing the Body Eclectic' – and this title, though never given more substance in the book, might stand as an assertion of one aspect at least of its cultural politics. Needless to add that the title parodies Walt Whitman's poem 'I Sing the Body Electric' and is therefore itself eclectic.

This, it seems to me, is one of the ways out of the dilemma posed in the book: that if all is parody, then any kind of cultural forgery is as good as another. Rushdie has read his Jameson, and knows the force of his critique of postmodernity; indeed, the argument is quoted to Saladin Chamcha by his fellow voice-over specialist, the Jewish actress Mimi Mamoulian:

> So comprehend, please, that I am an intelligent female. I have read *Finnegans Wake* and am conversant with postmodernist critiques of the West, e.g. that we have here a society capable only of pastiche: a 'flattened' world. When I become the voice of a bottle of bubble bath, I am entering Flatland knowingly, understanding what I'm doing and why. Viz., I am earning cash.
>
> (ibid.: 261)

Against this comprehensible cynicism, the aesthetics of Jumpy Joshi are based not upon any notion of authenticity or Palace of Art outside of Flatland, but upon the specific social and political solidarities that can be forged within it.

Equally, the novel has to confront the possibility that in Flatland, in a world drained of all effective personal and aesthetic contrasts by the relentless recycling of pastiche, the old generic intensities are no longer available, and the novel itself risks being reduced accordingly. Thus the tragic conclusion of the story is in danger of missing its mark:

What follows is tragedy. – Or, at the least the echo of tragedy, the full-blooded original being unavailable to modern men and women, so it's said. A burlesque for our degraded, imitative times, in which clowns re-enact what was first done by heroes and by kings.

(ibid.: 424)

But this is a danger that is perhaps scotched in its very recognition; or we can say that the force of the writing itself can reclaim the affective intensities of tragedy, however hedged about by burlesque. At all events, the novel does recover some of the force of tragedy in its conclusion, even if it occupies that generic space only briefly as it moves in and out of other generic possibilities. *Satanic Verses* sings the body eclectic to the end.

It can therefore be concluded that Salman Rushdie's novel is built up out of a cultural politics of parody that is placed very specifically in the fraught negotiations of migrant experience, though its comic ambitions are partly aimed at defusing the intensities of that experience, without in the least underestimating the necessities for political allegiances and solidarities. Yet all this is only meaningful in a cultural situation in which parody and its associated forms are recognised in the appropriate aesthetic way. The fate of the book, notoriously, has been that the parody of Islam has not been received as a playful exploration of the limits of sacred authority, but as a flagrant transgression of them. At the very least, this is a reminder of the fact that postmodernism, whether characterised by parody or pastiche, cannot be thought of as reaching into all the corners of the contemporary world.

A very different aesthetic of parody dominates another group of so-called 'postcolonial' novels, which are engaged in the business of 'writing back'; that is, they are doing what Jumpy Joshi announces in the titles of his poetry, taking the titles of cultural authority and turning them back against the metropolitan centres from where they issued: they are 'reclaiming the metaphor'.

A group of novels of this kind includes Jean Rhys's *Wide Sargasso Sea* (1966), J.M. Coetzee's *Foe* (1986) and Peter Carey's *Jack Maggs* (1997) – and this latter is the book that I choose briefly to discuss. For this novel rewrites *Great Expectations*, in fact is a structural parody of Dickens's novel. In a manner which recalls *Possession*, but issuing from a very different cultural politics, Carey invents an alternative version of early Victorian London, to which an Australian convict Jack Maggs returns in search of the young man whom he has been secretly benefiting. One of the people he encounters, and who mesmerises Maggs into recounting his life story, is the ambitious young novelist Tobias Oates. This latter is the son of a feckless father, married to an unsympathetic wife and enamoured of her younger sister; he is in a situation, in short, not entirely dissimilar from that of Dickens himself in 1837. Carey, in fact, has constructed a structural parody of *Great Expectations*, in which the returned Australian convict appears as a very much more threatening figure than in the hypotext, and in which the activity of the novelist appears as altogether more ambivalent in the manner in which it takes over the life stories of others.

There is little direct parody in the book, though it is clear that the novel that Tobias Oates will eventually publish, called *Jack Maggs*, will be a 'Newgate novel' (melodramatic novel of criminal life popular in the 1830s and 1840s), in the manner of Lytton's *Paul Clifford* or even Dickens's own *Oliver Twist*. The opening chapter of this parodied novel does indeed appear in Peter Carey's *Jack Maggs*:

> It was a dismal January day in the year of 1818, and the yellow fog which had lain low all morning lifted a moment in the afternoon and then, as if the desolate pile of rock and stone thereby revealed was far too melancholy a sight to be endured, it descended again like a shroud around the walls of Newgate Prison.
>
> These walls, being made from Welsh blue stone, had not been easily broken by the quarryman, and yet the fog, by virtue of its

persistence, had been able slowly to penetrate the stone's dark inhuman heart and touch the skin of a young woman prisoner who had fallen asleep with her face against her cell wall.

(Carey, 1998: 274)

The text continues in a similar manner for a several pages, combining self-conscious literary artifice with melodramatic contrasts. It is not clear that this manner of writing is simply repudiated, despite the parodic skill with which Carey captures the very particular idiom of the genre, best described as 'criminal Gothic'. In fact Carey's novel itself is a kind of contemporary Gothic, rediscovering some of the force of that nineteenth-century mode to deal with the nineteenth-century underworld which is partly the novel's topic. But the main force of the structural parody in the novel is to rewrite the story of *Great Expectations* in order to tilt the balance away from Pip towards Magwitch. Drawing on possible emphases within Dickens's novel, Magwitch/Maggs now appears as the victim of brutality and violence inflicted on him both in England and as a convict in Australia; his is a literal return of the repressed, in which the social victim created by English society and expelled by the state with unspeakable violence, returns to the 'home country' and threatens it with a reminder of the roots of its wealth. *Jack Maggs* is thus an attempt at narrative reconfiguration of the discursive order laid out in *Great Expectations*, and indeed other nineteenth-century novels, in which the Empire features as the inescapable margin surrounding representations of the metropolitan centre (see Said, 1994).

Another of Dickens's novels in which Australia features is, of course, *David Copperfield*, which appears unexpectedly at the end of *Jack Maggs*. Readers might recall that Mr Micawber makes a surprising success of his life after he has emigrated to Australia, becoming a leading citizen in the small town to which he takes himself and his family. This narrative conclusion is echoed in

Carey's novel, in which Maggs, instead of dying in flight like his prototype in *Great Expectations*, returns to Australia with a new wife to become the progenitor of a successful Australian clan. In fact, he turns out all along to have been a parody of Micawber as much as Magwitch, so that Carey rewrites Dickens's novels to claim the convict and not the scapegrace gentleman as Australian ancestor.

Satanic Verses, then, and *Jack Maggs*, suggest two different aspects of the politics of parody in postcolonial contexts. In the former novel, parody enters intimately into the formation of the self, and the problem for Salman Rushdie is to find a way of differentiating between this pervasive sense of mimicry or cultural assimilation, and out-and-out fakery. Culturally the book proposes a policy of 'historically validated eclecticism', which in artistic term would include 'reclaiming the metaphor'. Though this phrase occurs in Rushdie's novel, I interpret it as a politics of parody that is followed out more fully in novels such as *Jack Maggs*. While for the postmodernist novelists parody can figure as part of their relationship to the cultural past, pursued with varying degrees of playfulness, in this postcolonial context it figures as a game where the cultural stakes are potentially very serious.

'KARAOKE CULTURE'?

While recognising the pervasiveness of parody in contemporary culture, my conclusion to this chapter is, however, a modest one. At the level of high culture, architecture and possibly other arts, parody is one of the ways in which artists and writers can invoke the cultural past, or other contemporary discursive modes, to 'double-code' their understanding of the present. The particular ways in which individual writers manage this double-coding, and the particular relations that they have to their hypotexts, vary remarkably, and require careful and individual analysis; these attitudes, however, can include loving reconstruction as well as political outrage, more or less explicit structural parody as much as outright verbal imitation. Postmodernism in this context alludes to a variety of cultural practices whose only common characteristic is the inclusion of references to other discursive possibilities in a way that makes discourse itself a part of the topic of the art work. There is nothing here which has not been anticipated in the cultural practice of the past; this does not make *Tristram Shandy* a postmodernist book. These postmodernist works of art or of literature are not insignificant; they represent an important and indeed powerful current in contemporary culture, which can be inflected in different ways and in differing political directions; it is a current which includes some of the major cultural renegotiations of the present moment. But it is equally possible to list other modes, conventions and cultural productions which are in no sense 'postmodernist' and in which parody plays no part.

At the level of popular culture, similarly, I have suggested the remarkable presence of parody and related forms in the endless and voracious circulation of cultural material that characterises popular entertainment, to the extent that it can be spoken of as 'karaoke culture', locked in an obsessive recycling or revoicing, driven by no other logic than the need to fill those endless broadcast or satellite hours and those newspaper column inches. In a world without cultural hierarchies, parody here certainly is not – or not only – parody of the 'high' by the 'low', for it more typically fixes upon other products of popular culture itself, as one comedian parodies another, as pop musicians and disc jockeys sample and remix each other, as indeed karaoke itself offers the chance to mimic or act out the incessantly reproduced voices of popular music.

Just as the specific techniques of the postmodernist novel have mostly been anticipated in the history of the novel, so too the parodic practices of contemporary popular culture can often be found in the systems of popular entertainment in the nineteenth and early twentieth centuries. What is different about the present moment is the dominance and scale of penetration of the culture industries, made possible by specific technical innovations; this in itself is a massively important transformation. But also, just as I argued that the specific cultural politics of postmodernist practitioners varied widely, so that it is necessary to distinguish between, say, Malcolm Bradbury and Antonia Byatt, or between Salman Rushdie and Peter Carey, so too distinctions need to be preserved among the parodic practices of popular culture. Some of this parody is sharply directed at deflating self-importance, and is politically and socially pointed and telling. Other parody, meanwhile, is done simply for the fun of it. There is no general politics of parody; you cannot decide in advance whether it seeks to contain the new or to deflate the old. Equally, at the level of popular culture, no general decisions can be made in advance about the cultural value of parody. Karaoke too can be a mode of empowerment, if that does not seem too preposterous a claim for it: it permits people to assimilate and transform the productions of contemporary popular culture in a peculiarly intimate and powerful way. A hostile critic could doubtless assert that this assimilation would be better described as the uncritical internalisation of those cultural models; but then parody has always been liable to oscillate into and out of the critical attitude, and such oscillations are just as possible in karaoke.

CONCLUSION

I began this book with a reference to George Eliot, and I am tempted to conclude with her also. In one of the *Impressions of Theophrastus Such* (1881), called 'Debasing the Moral Currency', she makes the case against parody in extreme terms. The essay's title gives the clue to her argument: parody debases the moral currency, and recklessly threatens the very fabric of civilisation by ridiculing the precious cultural safeguards which are its highest achievements in art and literature. Eliot therefore abominates 'the burlesquing spirit which ranges to and fro and up and down the earth, seeing no reason (except a precarious censorship) why it should not appropriate every sacred, heroic, and pathetic theme which serves to make up the treasure of human admiration, hope, and love' (1881: 148). She invokes the recent revolutionary burning of the Tuileries Palace in Paris, and the Captain Swing riots of earlier in the century; parodists are compared to those *pétroleuses* and rioters, but their threat to civilisation is if anything more worrying by being less visible.

Despite the extravagance of the comparison, this is an argument which deserves to be taken seriously. At first sight it appears to confirm, by virtue of the seriousness with which it is proposed,

just that opposition between the sacred word and the carnivalesque energies of parody which is one of Bakhtin's fundamental
points. George Eliot, however, would appear to be on the oppos-
ing side from the Russian philosopher. By a curious twist, the
text of Bakhtin has now, in the early twenty-first century, become
the sacred word, and to question the value of the carnivalesque
genres, even if one has George Eliot as an ally, is to run counter to
the spirit of the age. Yet perhaps a more nuanced reading of
Bakhtin can lead us to a less indiscriminate cultural politics, in
which the choice before us is not such a straightforward either/or.

Bakhtin's most extensive account of carnival, and the parodic
forms which, he claims, accompany it, is to be found in the book
on Rabelais, which is very specifically tied to the late Middle
Ages and the Early Modern Period. While it is true that the
account can be generalised so as to describe societies at other (or
indeed all) historical periods, to do so is to lose the historical
specificity of Bakhtin's case, which sets out to describe the particular cultural dynamics of a society in transition – Rabelais's pro-
lific parodic energies are directed towards specific authoritative
targets. In fact, Bakhtin very particularly argues that in succeeding centuries the creative laughter of the Renaissance becomes
reduced, a merely negative affair which lacks the life-giving force
that it enjoys in the grotesque realism of Rabelais and Cervantes.
It follows from this general case that we cannot decide in advance
on the cultural politics of parody, but have to ask just what is
being parodied and from what perspective. We do not have to
choose between George Eliot and Bakhtin, but rather between
Cervantes and the chivalric romance, or between Southey and *The
Anti-Jacobin Review*, or between *Hello!* magazine and Jonathan
Coe's *What a Carve Up!*.

Nevertheless, while we always have to place parody within the
specific cultural practices of particular social and discursive formations, we can also recognise that the secular struggle between
the genres is in fact never-ending. The 'sacred word', to use the

Bakhtinian phrase, is constantly changing, and the social order, as it transforms itself over the centuries, is constantly discarding and reinventing that which it is prepared to consider 'sacred, heroic and pathetic'. Parody, we have seen, is one of the means by which this process is carried forward, whether or not the energies driving that process are popular or elite. Equally, parody can be one of the means by which the languages of out-groups are ridiculed, and new literary styles are attacked. Parody, despite George Eliot, can be a means employed by that 'precarious censorship' to keep a check on the strange, the challenging or simply the new. And here also we cannot decide in advance on its value; though it would certainly be an unattractive cultural politics which was always aligned with the voice of authority, to assign a singular political or social value to parody would be like trying to do the same for laughter.

So we confront finally the impossibility of that enterprise which has necessarily bedevilled discussions of parody: the effort to decide, one way or the other, what value to ascribe to the mode. It can no more be assigned a value than laughter itself, by which it is so often accompanied. Parody and the parodic forms more generally are inevitable manoeuvres in the to-and-fro of language, in the competition between genres, and in the unceasing struggle over meanings and values that make up any social order. Undoubtedly, at some historical moments and in some societies, parody has been more centrally present than at others. But the crucial questions remain: what cultural work is the parody effecting? On whose behalf is it working? With what wit and verve is the parody performed? None of these questions can be decided in advance, for all of them require an understanding of particular utterances in particular contexts. The pervasiveness of parody in the contemporary cultural moment requires just the same enthusiasm and scepticism as were necessary at the moment of mock-heroic at the beginning of the eighteenth century or the flowering of parody at the beginning of the nineteenth.

The temptation is to see parody as a parasitic mode, necessarily coming after the host text which it imitates or feeds upon. There is an evident truth in this common-sense perception – *Not the Nine O'Clock News* would make no sense unless *The Nine O'Clock News* preceded it. But the force of this perception needs to be tempered by two considerations, quite apart from any paradoxes that can be generated from thinking about the ambiguities of the host/parasite relationship. The first is that there is no unsullied point of origin, in which the hypotext existed without the contaminating presence of parody or the parodic forms: given the pervasiveness of parody in language use, most forms are going to be shot through with more or less mocking or derisive imitations or anticipations of the other's word. Second, the parodic paradox, by which parody creates new utterances out of the utterances that it seeks to mock, means that it preserves as much as it destroys – or rather, it preserves in the moment that it destroys – and thus the parasite becomes the occasion for itself to act as host. In this as in everything else, parody and its related forms serve to continue the conversation of the world, though its particular contribution is to ensure that the conversation will be usually carried on noisily, indecorously and accompanied by laughter.

GLOSSARY

burlesque Burlesque came into both French and English usage in the seventeenth century, deriving from the Italian *burla* meaning ridicule or mockery. This trajectory, from Italian through French into English, is significant in following the literary fashion for comic and mocking verse that the term described. In the seventeenth century, burlesque had the primary signification of 'merry' writing, and indeed became the generic term for different kinds of comic-parodic writing in the eighteenth century (see Bond, 1964). The particular association of burlesque with the comic persists to this day. In the theatre, the word has followed a different path, being used in the eighteenth century to describe a tradition of parodic anti-heroic drama, and in the nineteenth century broadened to describe lavish and miscellaneous entertainments for which such drama provided only the framework. As such, burlesque theatre was one of the forerunners of music hall and vaudeville. A more specialised American meaning for the word developed from one of the variety acts included on a typical burlesque bill; burlesque denotes the twentieth-century entertainment known in Britain as the striptease.

carnivalesque Following Bakhtin's (1984b) account of carnival in late Medieval and Renaissance Europe, the carnivalesque refers to all those cultural and literary practices which draw upon popular-festive energies to relativise or even to overturn the authority of the discourses of power and authority. Carnivalesque writing need have only the most distant relation to actual carnival festivities; it habitually sets multiple voices or discourses in play in ways which afford ultimate authority to none of them.

corrective function See **normative function**.

heteroglossia/heteroglossic Coinages of the Russian philosopher and literary critic, Mikhail Bakhtin (1981), to allude to the multiple 'languages' that are always present within an apparently unitary national language: dialects, professional jargons, slangs, accents, generational linguistic differences, and so on. For Bakhtin, this heteroglossic diversity is marked by various relations of prestige and authority, and is thus fertile ground for the parodic forms since these often pit one 'language' against another. See Bakhtin, *The Dialogic Imagination* (1981).

hudibrastic A word coined in the wake of Samuel Butler's poem *Hudibras* (1663–1678). Despite many imitations, *Hudibras* was effectively *sui generis* and certainly troubled seventeenth- and eighteenth-century criticism, which found it hard to fit it into its categories of low and high **burlesque**. The poem is comic and satiric, telling the story of a Presbyterian knight in a manner which recalls Cervantes; but while the poem is generally modelled on both romance and epic models, its particular appeal lies in its rollicking octosyllabic couplets, making much use of broken, double and even triple rhymes, and energetically switching from the grand to the demotic and back again. In this example, the female denizen of a provincial bear-baiting is described in an epic-style roll-call of heroes:

> At beating quarters up, or forage,
> Behav'd herself with matchless courage;
> And laid about a fight more busily,
> Then th'Amazonian Dame, Penthesile.
>
> (1, II, 375–8)

Hudibrastic can then be used to signify a general **travesty** (that is, a travesty which is directed at whole modes of writing rather than particular texts); but more usually it describes writing which attempts to use Butler's distinctive verse form for comic effect.

hypotext/hypertext Words coined by Gerard Genette in *Palimpsestes* (1982), to denote, respectively, the text upon which secondary writing is modelled, and the secondary text itself. The relationship of hypertext to hypotext need not be parodic, but includes all the forms of intertextual relationship, including **imitation**, **travesty**, **mock-heroic**, skit, and so forth

imitation In addition to its usual or common-sense meaning, imitation signifies a specific literary form widespread in the seventeenth and eighteenth centuries, in which a classical or other prestigious model is translated and rewritten with specific references to the contemporary world. Characteristically, imitations both call upon the authority of the imitated model to gain some purchase on the immediate moment, and set the skill and virtuosity of the modern poet into competition with those of the model. Examples of the imitation include Pope's 'Imitations of Horace'; and Johnson's 'London', an imitation of Juvenal's sixth satire, which transposes the situations of Rome and London.

intertextuality A word coined by Julia Kristeva to denote the transposition of any cultural or signifying practice into another, intertextuality has often been diminished in scope to signify no more than the reliance of any text upon writing that precedes it – in effect, to denote little more than source study. However, a more extensive usage persists, in which intertextuality refers to the constitution of any piece of writing out of the myriad codes, quotations and discursive fragments that surround it. A radical conclusion can be drawn from this: just as texts are constituted out of a mosaic of codes, so are their readers. Understanding intertextuality in this way can lead to the dissolution of any centred or unitary sense of the subject.

metafiction Fiction which has built into it a moment of self-reflection, or which alludes to its own, or others', fictional practice. Parodic novels which include parodies of other fictions tend to have a metafictional aspect, since they draw attention to the nature of story-telling in suggesting the inadequacy of the styles that they parody.

mock-heroic A particular poetic practice characteristic of neoclassical poetry both in France and England, mock-heroic uses the manner, style and diction of heroic verse with a contemporary or trivial subject-matter. The classic canon includes Dryden's *MacFlecknoe* (1682), Garth's *The Dispensary* (1714), and Pope's *The Rape of the Lock* (1712–14). Mock-heroic can range from the playful to the more decidedly satirical; it characteristically depends upon the incongruity between manner and matter, but its effects are the inverse of **travesty** – where the latter reduces, mock-heroic magnifies:

> *Sol* thro' white Curtains shot a tim'rous Ray,
> And op'd those Eyes that must eclipse the Day;
> Now lapdogs give themselves the rowzing Shake,
> And sleepless Lovers, just at Twelve, awake.
>
> (*Rape of the Lock*, 1, 13–16)

Mock-heroic frequently uses **parody** (understood in its eighteenth-century meaning of allusion or imitation) of heroic poetry to establish a comic distance between prestigious cultural context and trivial contemporary moment; this discrepancy permits a range of comic effects among which satire is only one. The mode (which spreads beyond poetry to become one of the characteristic tones of eighteenth-century writing) can be seen as a particular way of negotiating a cultural situation in which inherited prestigious forms continue to carry authority but can no longer convincingly be deployed unironically in the contemporary moment.

normative function/corrective function Parody which presupposes some norm by which the parodied forms are to be judged, exercises a normative function in seeking to re-establish the authority of that norm. It is thus

also corrective in seeking to correct the mistaken manner, style or attitudes of those writers who are parodied.

novelisation   By extending Bakhtin's account of the relationship of the
novel to the poetic genres, especially epic, novelisation can be used to
describe the progressive relativisation of, and scepticism towards, the
prestigious and sacred discourse of society. **Parody** is one of the principal
formal means which carries forward this process of novelisation. While it
is tempting to see this as a continuous process in the West from the late
Middle Ages onwards, it is better to see novelisation as more historical
and less epochal, as different social orders discard and rediscover sacred
or authoritative words.

parody   Deriving from the Ancient Greek παρῳδία, parody has accumu-
lated a range of differing meanings in its long history. In this book it is
used as the generic term for a range of related cultural practices, all of
which are imitative of other cultural forms, with varying degrees of mockery or humour. In Greek and then Latin usage, *parodia* signified a specific
form of mock poetry or ode, which used the manner and diction of the
high forms and applied them to a trivial topic. But it also denoted a more
widespread and more neutral practice of quotation and allusion. In neoclassical usage (seventeenth and eighteenth centuries), parody could
mean no more than an extended allusion to another writer included in a
longer work. The predominant modern usage defines parody as a mocking
imitation, but this usage is contested, with various efforts to return it,
first, to a more neutral or neoclassical usage in which the element of
mockery would be absent – in which case parody would be more like the
practice of **imitation** (Linda Hutcheon *A Theory of Parody: The Teachings
of Twentieth-Century Art Forms*, 1985), and, second, to reconnect it with
the fully comic practice of parody to be found in Rabelais's or Sterne's
writing (Margaret Rose, *Parody: Ancient, Modern and Post-modern*, 1993).
    A useful distinction can be made between *specific* and *general* parody.
The former consists of a parody of a specific art-work or piece of writing,
as in the following specific parody of Burns:

> Gin a body meet a body
> Flyin' through the air,
> Gin a body hit a body,
> Will it fly? and where?
>
>   (James Clerk Maxwell)

General parody, by contrast, takes as its **hypotext** not one specific work but a whole manner, style or discourse, sufficiently suggested by Byron's opening invocation to a Canto of *Don Juan*: 'Hail Muse! Etc. ...'. The practice of general parody is very close to **pastiche**, and indeed in both forms writers can move into and out of a satirical or ironic distance from the manner imitated.

pastiche   The French word *pastiche* has now largely replaced the Italian *pasticcio*, but in the eighteenth and nineteenth centuries the latter was actually the more usual term. In Italian, the word denotes a pie made of various ingredients; by metaphorical extension principally to art and music criticism, *pasticcio* or *pastiche* denoted a musical medley or pot-pourri, or a picture made up of fragments pieced together. It is in painting that the term began to take on the meaning of imitation of another style without critical distance, and it is this meaning that has come to dominate in contemporary usage of the term. In literary usage, pastiche denotes the more or less extended imitation of the style or manner of another writer or literary period.

   The term pastiche has been given particular currency by Fredric Jameson in the essay 'Postmodernism, or The Cultural Logic of Late Capitalism', in which he distinguishes pastiche from **parody** on the grounds that pastiche takes no critical distance from the material it recycles: pastiche, in fact, is 'blank parody'. Pastiche is then seen as characteristic of postmodernism and thus expresses the cultural logic of late capitalism, since the absolute extension of the commodity system prevents the recourse to any discourse of nature or tradition (as in earlier Modernism) which could be used to measure or ironise the forms that are pastiched.

spoof   A hoaxing game invented by the comedian Arthur Roberts, the meaning of spoof has been extended to make it in effect a demotic synonym for **parody**, though it retains a strong sense of the original meaning of hoax. Thus while spoof can certainly mean no more than parody, it can also denote a mocking imitation which is deliberately meant to deceive readers, listeners or viewers. Classic spoofs for British television viewers or newspaper readers are the 1960s' *Panorama* documentary describing the harvesting of spaghetti from trees, and the 1980s' special supplement of *The Guardian* newspaper devoted to the island of San Serif. Both these spoofs were broadcast or published on 1 April.

travesty   Like **burlesque**, travesty is a term that became current in the seventeenth century, both in English and French, and derived from an Italian word, *travestare*, to disguise. Indeed, the terms were not always clearly differentiated. Travesty, however, has come to denote specifically a reductive or diminishing mode, which translates a particular high-prestige literary model into low demotic or coarse accents. The most famous examples of travesty are thus Scarron's *Virgile Travesti* and Cotton's English imitation of it, the *Scarronides* (1664) – characterised by Dryden as 'dull burlesque', in which '*Parnassus* spoke the cant of *Billingsgate*'. Such effects of transition from the 'high' to the 'low', from the dignified to the base, are characteristic of travesty, as the first two lines of Cotton's *Scarronides* sufficiently indicate:

> I Sing the man, (read it who list,
> A *Trojan* true as ever pist).

The modern meaning, of a ludicrously or deliberately insufficient imitation ('a travesty of justice'), is derived from this earlier literary usage.

NOTES

1 APPROACHES TO PARODY

1   For a developed account of the meanings of these parodies, see John Drakakis, 'Shakespeare in quotations', in *Studying British Culture: An Introduction*, edited by Susan Bassnett (London: Routledge, 1997), pp. 152–72.

2   For Russian Formalist accounts of parody, see Victor Erlich, *Russian Formalism: History-Doctrine* (The Hague: Mouton, 1965), p. 257 ff.; Jurij Tynyanov, 'On literary evolution', in *Readings in Russian Poetics: Formalist and Structuralist Views*, edited by Ladislav Matejka and Krystyna Pomorska (Ann Arbor, MI: the University of Michigan Press, 1978), pp. 66–77; Roman Jakobson, 'The dominant', in ibid., pp. 82–7; Viktor Shklovsky, 'A parodying novel: Sterne's *Tristram Shandy*, in *Laurence Sterne: A Collection of Critical Essays*, edited by John Traugott (Englewood Cliffs, NJ: Prentice-Hall, 1968); and Viktor Shklovsky, 'The connection between devices of syuzhet construction and general stylistic devices', in *Russian Formalism: A Collection of Articles and Texts in Translation*, edited by Stephen Bann and John E. Bowlt (Edinburgh: Scottish Academic Press, 1973), pp. 48–72.

2 PARODY IN THE ANCIENT AND MEDIEVAL WORLDS

1   'Homer's Battle of the Frogs and Mice', in Thomas Parnell, *Collected Poems of Thomas Parnell* (Newark: University of Delaware Press, 1989).

2   For an interesting modern attempt at a satyr play, which is based upon the discovery of satyric fragments (of Sophocles' *Ichneutae*) at Oxyrinchus in 1907, see Tony Harrison's *The Trackers of Oxyrinchus* (London: Faber and Faber, 1990).

3   See Peter Burke, *Popular Culture in Early Modern Europe* (London: Temple Smith, 1978), p. 192; Ingvild Salid Gilhus, 'Carnival in religion: the Feast of Fools in France', *Numen: International Review for the History of Religions*, 37 (1990), pp. 24–52.

3 PARODY IN THE NOVEL

1   For an account of the novel as generically defined by its repudiation of romance, see Maurice Z. Shroder, 'The novel as a genre', in *The*

Theory of the Novel, edited by Philip Stevick (New York: The Free Press, 1967), pp. 11–29. More generally, the Lukacsian history of the novel as the form of 'lost illusions', or the Leavisian emphasis upon 'maturity' within the genre, both lend themselves to reductive assimilations of the kind I set forth in this one-sided history of the novel.

4 PARODY AND POETRY

1 Noel Malcolm, *The Origins of English Nonsense* (London: HarperCollins, 1997), p. 30. This account of seventeenth-century nonsense writing (which includes an anthology) is very important in correcting the fixation on the nineteenth-century writing of Lewis Carroll and Edward Lear. Its importance can be gauged by comparing it with Geoffrey Grigson's (very enjoyable) *Faber Book of Nonsense Verse* (London: Faber and Faber, 1979), which takes scarcely any of its examples from the seventeenth century. Many of Grigson's examples are really parodies.

5 THE BEAUTIES OF BURLESQUE

1 See Simon Trussler, in the introduction to *Chrononhotonthologos*, in *Burlesque Plays of the Eighteenth Century* (London: Oxford University Press, 1969), p. 209. See also the entry on Quin in Phyllis Hartnoll (ed.), *The Oxford Companion to the Theatre* (London: Oxford University Press, 1967).
2 See Brean S. Hammond, *Professional Imaginative Writing in England, 1670–1740: 'Hackney for Bread'* (Oxford: Clarendon Press, 1997), p. 253.

BIBLIOGRAPHY

Adam, J.A.S. and White, B.C. (eds) (1912) *Parodies and Imitations Old and New*, with a Preface by Arthur Quiller-Couch, London: Hutchinson.

Anderson, P. (1998) *The Origins of Postmodernity*, London: Verso.

Aristophanes (1964) *The Wasps, The Poet and the Women, The Frogs*, translated with an Introduction by D. Barret, London: Penguin.

Bakhtin, M. (1981) *The Dialogic Imagination: Four Essays*, ed. M. Holquist, trans. C. Emerson and M. Holquist, Austin, TX: University of Texas Press.

—— (1984a) *Problems of Dostoevsky's Poetics*, ed. and trans. C. Emerson, Manchester: Manchester University Press.

—— (1984b) *Rabelais and His World*, trans. H. Iswolsky, Bloomington, IND: Indiana University Press.

Barber, C.L. (1959) *Shakespeare's Festive Comedies*, Princeton, NJ: Princeton University Press.

Bate, J. (1985) 'Parodies of Shakespeare', *Journal of Popular Culture* 19, 75–89.

—— (1998) *The Cure for Love*, London: Picador.

Bayless, M. (1996) *Parody in the Middle Ages: The Latin Tradition*, Ann Arbor, MI: University of Michigan Press.

Beaumont, F. and Fletcher, J. (1875) *The Knight of the Burning Pestle*, in J.S. Keltie (ed.) *British Dramatists*, London: William P. Nimmo.

Beerbohm, M. (1993) *A Christmas Garland*, New Haven and London: Yale University Press.

Bennett, D. (1985) 'Parody, postmodernism, and the politics of reading', *Critical Quarterly* 27, 27–43.

Bond, R.P. (1964) *English Burlesque Poetry 1700–1750*, New York: Russell and Russell.

Booth, M.R. (1976) *English Plays of the Nineteenth Century*, vol. V, *Pantomimes, Extravaganzas and Burlesques*, Oxford: Clarendon Press.

Boswell, J. (1867) *The Life of Samuel Johnson, LL.D.*, London: Routledge.

Bradbury, M. (1976) *Who Do You Think You Are?*, London: Penguin.

—— (1987) 'An age of parody: style in the modern arts', in *No, Not Bloomsbury*, London: André Deutsch.

Brett, S. (1984) *The Faber Book of Parodies*, London: Faber and Faber.

Broich, U. (1990) *The Eighteenth-Century Mock-heroic Poem*, trans. D.H. Wilson, Cambridge: Cambridge University Press.

Burke, P. (1978) *Popular Culture in Early Modern Europe*, London: Temple Smith.

Burnand, F.C. (1866) *Paris, or Vive Lemprière: An Original Burlesque*, London: T.H. Lacy.

Byatt, A. (1991) *Possession; A Romance*, London: Chatto and Windus.

Caesar, T. (1984) '"I quite forget what – say a daffodilly": Victorian parody', *English Literary History* 51, 795–818.

Calverley, C.S. (1904) *Verses, Translations and Fly Leaves*, London: George Bell and Sons.

Carey, H. (1729) *Poems on Several Occasions*, London, reproduced from the English Poetry Full-Text Database published by Chadwyck-Healey Ltd.

Carey, P. (1998) *Jack Maggs*, London: Faber and Faber.

Cervantes, M. de (1981) *Don Quixote*, the Ormsby translation, ed. J.R. Jones and K. Douglas, New York and London: Norton.

Chambers, E.K. (1903) *The Mediaeval Stage*, 2 vols, Oxford: Oxford University Press.

Clinton-Baddeley, V.C. (1952) *The Burlesque Tradition in English Theatre after 1660*, London: Methuen.

Coe, J. (1995) *What a Carve Up!*, London: Penguin.

Coleridge, S.T. (1973) *Poetical Works*, ed. E.H. Coleridge, London: Oxford University Press.

Cope, W. (1986) *Making Cocoa for Kingsley Amis*, London: Faber and Faber.

Cotton, C. (1667) *Scarronides: or, Virgile Travestie. A Mock-Poem, On the First and Fourth Books of Virgils Ænæis in English, Burlésque,*

London, reproduced from the English Poetry Full-Text Database published by Chadwyck-Healey Ltd.

Dane, J.A. (1980) 'Parody and satire: a theoretical model', *Genre* 13, 145–59.

Dentith, S. (1995) *Bakhtinian Thought: An Introductory Reader*, London: Routledge.

Dickens, C. (1971) *Bleak House*, Harmondsworth: Penguin.

Docker, J. (1994) *Postmodernism and Popular Culture: A Cultural History*, Cambridge University Press: Cambridge.

Dowling, M.G. (1834) *Othello Travestie: An Operatic Burlesque Burletta*, London: T.H. Lacy.

Drakakis, J. (1997) 'Shakespeare in quotations', in S. Bassnett (ed.) *Studying British Culture, An Introduction*, London: Routledge.

Dryden, J. (1972) 'The art of poetry', in H.T. Swedenberg Jr. (ed.) *Works of John Dryden*, vol. II, *Poems 1681–1684*, Berkeley, CA: University of California Press.

Eliot, G. (1881) *Impressions of Theophrastus Such*, Edinburgh: Blackwood.

—— (1973) 'The Sad Fortunes of the Rev. Amos Barton', in *Scenes of Clerical Life*, Harmondsworth: Penguin.

—— (1988) *Middlemarch*, Oxford: Oxford University Press.

Eliot, T.S. (1963) *Collected Poems 1909–1962*, London: Faber and Faber.

Erlich, V. (1965) *Russian Formalism: History-Doctrine*, The Hague: Mouton.

Ermarth, E.D. (ed.) (1992) *Sequel to History: Postmodernism and the Crisis of Representational Time*, Princeton, NJ: Princeton University Press.

Euripides (1959) *The Cyclops*, translated with an Introduction by William Arrowsmith, in D. Grene and R. Lattimore (eds) *The Complete Greek Tragedies*, vol. III, *Euripides*, Chicago: University of Chicago Press.

Fielding, H. (1963) *Joseph Andrews* and *Shamela*, ed. A.R. Humphreys, London: Dent.

—— (1980) *The History of Tom Jones*, ed. R.P.C. Mutter, Harmondsworth: Penguin.

Fitts, D. (1962) 'Translator's Preface' to *Ladies Day*, in Aristophanes, *Four Comedies: Lysistrata, The Frogs, The Birds, Ladies Day*, trans. D. Fitts, New York: Harcourt, Brace and World.

Flaubert, G. (1972) *Madame Bovary*, Paris: Gallimard.

Foote, S. and Murphy, A. (1984) *Plays by Samuel Foote and Arthur Murphy*, ed. G. Taylor, Cambridge: Cambridge University Press.

Garth, S. (1714) *The Dispensary*, Tonson, London, reproduced from the English Poetry Full-Text Database published by Chadwyck-Healey Ltd.

Gay, J. (1926) *The Poetical Works of John Gay*, ed. G.C. Faber, London; reproduced from the English Poetry Full-Text Database published by Chadwyck-Healey Ltd.

Genette, G. (1982) *Palimpsestes: La Littérature au Second Degré*, Paris: Éditions du Seuil.

Gilbert, S. (1969) *James Joyce's* Ulysses: *A Study*, Harmondsworth: Penguin.

Gilhus, I.S. (1990) 'Carnival in religion: the Feast of Fools in France', *Numen: International Review for the History of Religion* 37, 24–52.

Grigson, G. (1979) (ed.) *Faber Book of Nonsense Verse*, London: Faber and Faber.

Halperin, J. (1986) *The Life of Jane Austen*, Brighton: Harvester Wheatsheaf.

Hamilton, W. (1951) 'Introduction', in Plato, *The Symposium*, London: Penguin.

—— (1884–9) (ed.) *Parodies of the Works of English and American Authors*, 6 vols, London: Reeves and Turner.

Hammond, B.S. (1997) *Professional Imaginative Writing in England, 1670–1740: 'Hackney for Bread'*, Oxford: Clarendon Press.

Harrison, T. (1990) *The Trackers of Oxyrinchus*, London: Faber and Faber.

Hartnoll, P. (ed.) (1967) *The Oxford Companion to the Theatre*, London: Oxford University Press.

Harvey, P. (ed.) (1967) *The Oxford Companion to English Literature*, 4th edition, Oxford: Oxford University Press.

Householder, F.W. Jr. (1944) 'ΠΑΡΩΙΔΙΑ', *Classical Philology* 39, 1–9.

Hutcheon, L. (1985) *A Theory of Parody: The Teachings of Twentieth-Century Art Forms*, London: Methuen.

—— (1988) *A Poetics of Postmodernism: History, Theory, Fiction*, London: Routledge.

—— (1994) *Irony's Edge*, London: Routledge.

Jakobson, R. (1978) 'The dominant', in L. Matejka and K. Pomorska (eds) *Readings in Russian Poetics: Formalist and Structuralist Views*, Ann Arbor, MI: University of Michigan Press.

Jameson, F. (1984) 'Postmodernism, or the cultural logic of late capitalism', *New Left Review* 146, 53–92.

—— (1988), 'The politics of theory: ideological positions in the postmodernism debate', in *The Ideologies of Theory; Essays 1971–1986*, vol. 2, *The Syntax of History*, London: Routledge.

Jencks, C. (1991) *The Language of Post-Modern Architecture*, 6th edition, London: Academy Editions.

Jerrold, W. and Leonard, R.M. (eds) (1913) *A Century of Parody and Imitation*, London: Oxford University Press.

Johnson, S. (1964) *The Yale Edition of the Works of Samuel Johnson*, vol. 6, *Poems*, ed. E.L. McAdam, New Haven and London: Yale University Press.

Jonson, B. (1967) *The Poetaster*, in *The Complete Plays*, 2 vols, London: Dent.

Joyce, J. (1968) *Ulysses*, Harmondsworth: Penguin.

Jump, J.D. (1972) *Burlesque*, London: Methuen.

Karrer, W. (1997) 'Cross-dressing between travesty and parody', in B. Müller (ed.) *Parody: Dimensions and Perspectives*, Amsterdam.

Keizer, T.A (1998) *The New Statesman* 3 July, p.53.

Kitchin, G. (1931) *A Survey of Burlesque and Parody in English*, Edinburgh: Oliver and Boyd.

Kristeva, J. (1974) *La Révolution du Langage Poétique*, Paris: Éditions du Seuil.

—— (1980) 'Word, dialogue and novel', in L.S. Roudiez (ed.) *Desire in Language: A Semiotic Approach to Literature and Art*, trans. T. Gora, A. Jardine and L. Roudiez, Oxford: Basil Blackwell.

Lawler, D. (1811) *The Earls of Hammersmith, or The Cellar Spectre, A Comical Tragical Burlesque Drama*, London: J. Duncombe.

Lessing, D. (1962) *The Golden Notebook*, London: Michael Joseph.

Lucian (1991) *A Selection*, edited with an Introduction, Translation and Commentary by M.D. MacLeod, Warminster: Aris and Philips.

Macdonald, D. (ed.) (1985) *Parodies; An Anthology from Chaucer to Beerbohm – and After*, with a new Introduction by V. Geng, New York: Da Capo Press.

Malcolm, N. (1997) *The Origins of English Nonsense*, London: HarperCollins.

Markiewicz, H. (1967) 'On the definitions of literary parody', in *To Honor Roman Jakobson: Essays on the Occasion of His Seventieth Birthday*, vol. 2, The Hague: Mouton.

Marlowe, C. (1969) *The Second Part of Tamburlaine the Great, in The Plays of Christopher Marlowe*, London: Oxford University Press.

Müller, B. (ed.) (1997) *Parody: Dimensions and Perspectives*, Amsterdam: Rodopi.

Nash, W. (1985) *The Language of Humour; Style and Technique in Comic Discourse*, London and New York: Longman.

Norwood, G. (1964) *Greek Comedy*, London: Methuen.

O'Hara, D.T. (1992) *Radical Parody: American Culture and Critical Agency After Foucault*, New York: Columbia University Press.

Parnell, T. (1989) *Collected Poems of Thomas Parnell*, Newark: University of Delaware Press.

Petronius (1977) *The Satyricon*, trans. J.P. Sullivan, Harmondsworth: Penguin.

Phiddian, R. (1995) *Swift's Parody*, Cambridge: Cambridge University Press.

Philips, A. (1937) *The Poems of Ambrose Philips*, ed. M.G. Segar, Oxford; reproduced from the English Poetry Full-Text Database published by Chadwyck-Healey Ltd.

Planché, J.R. (1986) *Plays by James Robinson Planché*, ed. D. Roy, Cambridge: Cambridge University Press.

Plato (1951) *The Symposium*, London: Penguin.

Poirier, R. (1968) 'The politics of self-parody', *The Partisan Review* 35:3, 339–53.

Poole, J. (1812) *Hamlet Travestie*, London: T.H. Lacy.

Pope, A. (1968) *The Poems of Alexander Pope*, ed. J. Butt, London: Methuen.

—— (1986) *Peri Bathous, or, Of the Art of Sinking in Poetry*, in R. Cowley (ed.) *The Prose Writings of Alexander Pope*, vol. II, *The Major Works, 1725–44*, Oxford: Blackwell.

Pound, E. (1968) *Collected Shorter Poems*, London: Faber and Faber.

Rabelais, F. (n.d.) *The Works of Rabelais*, faithfully translated from the French, and illustrated by G. Doré, printed for private circulation, Nottingham.

Rawson, C. (1985) *Order from Confusion Sprung: Studies in Eighteenth-Century Literature from Swift to Cowper*, London: George Allen and Unwin.

Relihan, J.C (1993) *Ancient Menippean Satire*, Baltimore and London: Johns Hopkins University Press.

Riewald, J.G (1966) 'Parody as criticism', *Neophilologus* 50, 126–48.

Roberts, R. (1971) *The Classic Slum: Salford Life in the First Quarter of the Century*, Manchester: Manchester University Press.

Rogers, P. (1980) *Hacks and Dunces; Pope, Swift and Grub Street*, London: Methuen.

Rose, M. (1979) *Parody/Metafiction: An Analysis of Parody as a Critical Mirror to the Writing and Reception of Fiction*, London: Croom Helm.

—— (1993) *Parody: Ancient, Modern and Post-modern*, Cambridge: Cambridge University Press.

Rushdie, S. (1992) *The Satanic Verses*, Delaware: The Consortium.

Said, E. (1994) *Culture and Imperialism*, New York: Knopf.

Seneca (1977) *The Apocolocyntosis*, trans. J.P. Sullivan, Harmondsworth: Penguin.

Shakespeare, W. (1951a) *As You Like It*, in P. Alexander (ed.) *The Complete Works*, London: Collins.

—— (1951b) *Hamlet*, in P. Alexander (ed.) *The Complete Works*, London: Collins.

—— (1951c) *Love's Labour's Lost*, in P. Alexander (ed.) *The Complete Works*, London: Collins.

—— (1951d) *A Midsummer Night's Dream*, in P. Alexander (ed.) *The Complete Works*, London: Collins.

Sharratt, B. (1984) *The Literary Labyrinth; Contemporary Critical Discourses*, Brighton: Harvester.

Shaw, G.B. (1937) *The Admirable Bashville, or Constancy Unrewarded*, in *The Complete Plays of Bernard Shaw*, London: Odhams Press.

Sheridan, R.B. (1975) *Sheridan's Plays*, ed. C. Price, London: Oxford University Press.

Shklovsky, V. (1968) 'A parodying novel: Sterne's *Tristram Shandy*, in J. Traugott (ed.) *Laurence Sterne: A Collection of Critical Essays*, Englewood Cliffs, NJ: Prentice-Hall.

—— (1973) 'The connection between devices of syuzhet construction and general stylistic devices', in S. Bann and J.E. Bowlt (eds) *Russian Formalism: A Collection of Articles and Texts in Translation*, Edinburgh: Scottish Academic Press.

Shroder, M.Z. (1967) 'The novel as a genre', in P. Stevick (ed.) *The Theory of the Novel*, New York: The Free Press.

Southey, R. (1909) *The Poems of Robert Southey*, ed. M.H. Fitzgerald, London: Henry Frowde.

Spark, M. (1963) *The Girls of Slender Means*, London: Macmillan.

Sterne, L. (1997) *The Life and Opinions of Tristram Shandy, Gentleman*, ed. M. New and J. New, London: Penguin.

Sutton, D.F. (1980) *The Greek Satyr Play*, Meisenheim am Glan: Verlag Anton Hain.

Tagholm, R. (1996) *Poems Not on the Underground: A Parody*, ed. 'Straphanger', Moreton-in-Marsh: Windrush Press.

Talfourd, F. (1848) *Macbeth, Somewhat removed from the text of Shakespeare*, London: T.H. Lacy.

Talfourd, F. and Byron, H.J. (1860) *The Miller and his Men*, London: T.H. Lacy.

Thackeray, W.M. (1877a) 'Barbazure', in *The Works of William Makepeace Thackeray*, vol. 8, London: Smith, Elder and Co.

—— (1877b) 'Rebecca and Rowena', in *The Works of William Makepeace Thackeray*, vol. 8, London: Smith, Elder and Co.

—— (1983) *Vanity Fair*, ed. J. Sutherland, Oxford: Oxford University Press.

Thomson, C. and Pagès, A. (eds) (1989) *Dire la Parodie: Colloque de Cerisy*, New York: Peter Lang.

Trussler, S. (ed.) (1969) *Burlesque Plays of the Eighteenth Century*, London: Oxford University Press.

Tynyanov, J. (1978) 'On literary evolution', in L. Matejka and K. Pomorska, (eds) *Readings in Russian Poetics: Formalist and Structuralist Views*, Ann Arbor, MI: University of Michigan Press.

Vološinov, V.N. (1976) *Freudianism: A Marxist Critique*, trans. L. Matejka and I.R. Titunik, New York: Academic Press.

—— (1986) *Marxism and the Philosophy of Language*, trans. L. Matejka and I.R. Titunik, New York: Academic Press.

Waugh, E. (1943) *Scoop*, Harmondsworth: Penguin.

INDEX

DATE DUE